TO ISABEL, MY MUM

THE SPANISH
HOME KITCHEN

JOSÉ PIZARRO

Hardie Grant

BOOKS

Although I love the adrenaline running through my veins during service in the restaurant, I also love cooking more quietly at home for friends and family. I started cooking in my twenties, but when I was a boy I was not allowed to be in the kitchen much at all; my mum was so busy helping my dad on the farm. Having breakfast, lunch and dinner on the table everyday at the right time was her way of showing her love. I always found a way to be in the kitchen though, absorbing the atmosphere, and taking in all the lovely smells that wafted through the air. Now all it takes is a subtle smell of chickpeas or a stew to take me right back to those moments of watching my mum and grandmother cooking at home in their rustic kitchens so full of love and life. Recipes capture moments like photographs, but even more than that, they allow us to recreate those same taste and smell sensations.

For me, cooking is so much about memories. I love people, and creating moments of happiness together is why I love to cook. When I return to a certain dish or recipe, all the memories about the people, places, and moments associated with it come flooding back, and add a pleasurable dimension. Memories make happiness.

"The memory of happiness is perhaps also happiness."

AGNÈS VARDA

A whole host of wonderful food-related memories are invoked every time I cook. Whenever I put a particular combination of ingredients together in a pan or on a plate I remember something from the past – happy memories of family and friends, remembering where we were or what we were doing, remembering what we were talking or laughing about, or just appreciating the time we spent together – this is the best thing about food.

The memories we have are just the surface though. Most of the time the real story of a dish goes way back, and has been passed from person to person, and from generation to generation, until here we are sitting in front of the dish ourselves. How extraordinary is that?

"Memories of life in old rural worlds live on in the cooking like ghosts hovering in saucepans."

CLAUDIA RODEN

I have always had so much respect for food historians who research, catalogue and preserve recipes. Their work helps me to be mindful of the responsibility we have to guard traditional recipes so they survive long into the future. In a way, I am doing this through writing this book. As a chef it is also my responsibility to develop and build on recipes so they improve. The languages we speak are not the same as they were hundreds of years ago, and neither are recipes the same, they've evolved too.

In this book I want to convey how important memories are in cooking, how we are recreating and creating each time we cook a dish and add the ingredient of a certain memory. In fact, memories are essential ingredients in my cooking. The most precious memories stay with us throughout our lives - this brings immense happiness. It's these most treasured and valuable memories that I strive to recreate at home, in my restaurants, and in my books.

I hope you can sense something of the tremendously happy memories behind the recipes in this book, and in turn that you'll be able to create some special memories of your own – these are real treasures.

"Memories are essential ingredients in my cooking."

JOSÉ PIZARRO

1

2

3

4

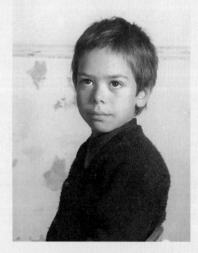

1. Baby José

2. José and Peter at Kew Gardens, London

3. José's parents, Antonio and Isabel, at José's sister Wedding in 1992

4. School photo of José at five years old

5. Jose's father Antonio in 1957

6. Jose's mother Isabel in 1957

7. Family trip to London in 2005

8. José and Peter at Zahara de los Atunes in 2021

9. The first time José and Peter met their dogs, Conchi and Pie

5

6

7

9

8

10. Jose's family visit to London

11. José's father, Antonio, photoshoot of *Seasonal Spanish Food*, José's first book

12. José and Isabel in Talaván

13. First communion of Juan, José's nephew, in 2004

14. José's parents' trip to Rome

15. José and Peter with Conchi and Pie in London, 2020, portrait taken by Tracey Emin

16. Peter and José with their niece Carmen at the *Andalusia* book launch in London at the Spanish Embassy in 2019

13

14

15

16

VEGETABLES

Living on a farm in rural Spain, my family knew how to live off the land. This is something that was passed down from generation to generation. My dad taught my older brother Antonio how to look after the allotments and how to get the best results. As my parents got older, we'd visit the *huerta* (vegetable garden) on a daily basis with them to see how the plants were doing, and which fresh produce was ready to pick. I have wonderful memories of walking to the garden with my dad: the experience of picking something as simple as a fresh tomato, ripened in the hot Extremadura sun, will always remain with me. My dad would sometimes scold me: 'No, don't pick that, son. It's not ready. Tomorrow it will be ready!' He was always right. He knew the produce he was growing so well he could tell you the exact moment each vegetable was ready to be picked and taken back to the kitchen table – not a moment too soon, nor too late!

I remember my poor dad coming to London for the first time in 2000: he couldn't believe the pitiful size, bitter taste, and sky-high price of the lemons here! In Spain, lemons are so plentiful they just fall from the trees and are everywhere on the ground. When ripened by the sun, they are juicy and a darker yellow, and they're not bitter at all. I remember him visiting Borough Market, too, where he encountered cherry tomatoes for the first time – he took some back to Spain with him and used the seeds to propagate his own plants. He was a gardener, through and through.

One of the main things I love about vegetables is how seasonal they are, and how the food we eat changes through the year depending on what's available in nature. For example, when you think of pumpkins, you immediately think of autumn and all its festivities, while the thought of blood oranges conjures up winter. In my restaurants, I like to change the menus to reflect the changing seasons and the variations in produce. This reminds me how dependent we are on our beautiful planet for existence, and it helps me feel more in touch with nature.

When I arrived in the UK from Spain in 1998, the vegetarian movement here was developing, and this was a new concept to me. The idea of vegetarianism really didn't exist in Spain at all at that time. At one point, I travelled back to Spain for an article I was doing about jamón Ibérico. The photographer I travelled with was vegetarian, and I remember the old lady who was cooking lunch for us on the farm we visited insisted the photographer could eat the jamón because the pigs were 100 per cent Ibéricio acorn-fed – and she wasn't joking! She really understood that a vegetarian was concerned that the *animal* had eaten vegetables. Anyway, my friend didn't eat the meat, and we found a great alternative. I have to say that I do really love vegetarian cuisine, and there are some spectacular vegetable-only dishes out there. I've watched closely how much this way of cooking and eating has evolved, and am so impressed with the creativity you see in this area. As a chef, it's always good to be challenged to create new things, and I really enjoy coming up with new recipes using vegetables alone.

TOMATO SOUP WITH FIGS

This is like the tomato soup we used to have when we were children. I have come across many different recipes over the years, but this one is closest to my heart. It is really simple, but – and this is a big but – you need the best tomatoes you can find. They need to be really ripe, and preferably grown and ripened under the sun. There's a real interplay between the sun and tomatoes – they just don't smell or taste the same if they're forced.

Life is full of great memories, and there's nothing better than breaking bread with the people you love. Enjoying this tomato soup with my family, made with tomatoes and figs from my dad's own vegetable garden, is a beautiful and emotional memory for me. To think of him planting, growing and picking the fruit by hand, then passing it to my mum for her to make this favourite dish, brings a tear to my eye – happy tears, of course; tears of joy, gratitude and love.

INGREDIENTS

2 tablespoons olive oil
1 small onion, finely chopped
2 garlic cloves, finely sliced
800 g (1 lb 12 oz) ripe tomatoes, roughly chopped
3 fresh oregano sprigs, leaves picked
400 ml (13 fl oz/generous 1½ cups) fresh vegetable stock
4 slices of slightly stale bread
3 very ripe figs, roughly chopped
extra virgin olive oil, for drizzling
sea salt and freshly ground black pepper

Heat the olive oil in a deep sauté pan over a medium heat. Add the onion and fry for 10 minutes until softened. Add the garlic and tomatoes and season well, then cook over a high heat for 5 minutes until they start to colour and break down.

Add the most of the oregano and fry for 1 minute more, then pour in the stock. Bring to a simmer and cook for 10 minutes until you have a rich, chunky tomato soup.

Put a slice of bread into the bottom of each bowl and pour the soup on top, allowing it to soak in. Scatter over the figs and remaining oregano leaves, then season and drizzle with extra virgin olive oil and serve.

BROAD BEAN TORTILLA

We have a saying in Extremadura: *'iHabas en Abril empiezan y en Abril acaban!'* ('Broad beans start in April, and finish in April!'). We mean that, for just that month, we have the best of the broad (fava) beans in Spain. The season is different in the UK, of course. When the broad bean pods are as long as your little finger, they are ready for this recipe. Keeping the beans inside, give the whole pods a good wash under the fresh spring water fountain in your village (oh, OK, or under your tap at home), and they're ready. Remember, you're not taking the beans out of the pods at this tender age. Just slice the whole pod – and you do need to slice them very finely. They're so good, so sweet and so yummy. In Spain, you can get very young canned broad beans preserved in extra virgin olive oil. If you can get those, they would also work for this recipe: just be sure to drain them well (you can use their oil for dipping).

INGREDIENTS

150 ml (5 fl oz/scant ⅔ cup) extra virgin olive oil, plus extra for drizzling
1 onion, very finely sliced
2 garlic cloves, finely chopped
500 g (1 lb 2 oz) baby broad (fava) beans in their pods, sliced
5 free-range eggs
sea salt and freshly ground black pepper

Pour 75 ml (2½ fl oz/5 tablespoons) of the olive oil into a large frying pan (skillet) over a low–medium heat and cook the onion for 10 minutes until really lovely and soft. Increase the heat to high and add the garlic and broad beans. Cook for 5 minutes until tender and golden. Remove from the heat and set aside.

In a bowl, beat the eggs, then add the still-warm broad bean mixture and plenty of seasoning.

Pour the remaining olive oil into an 18-cm (7-in) deep non-stick frying pan over a high heat. When the oil is hot, add the egg mixture. Swirl the pan until the mixture starts to set around the edges, then reduce the heat to low and cook for 4–5 minutes, until the tortilla just starts to set, so the bottom and sides are golden, but the middle is still quite loose.

Cover the pan with a flat lid or board and turn the tortilla carefully on to it. Don't worry that it is still quite runny: it will all come back together when you continue to cook it. Slide the tortilla back into the pan and, over a low heat, use a spatula to tuck the edges under to give it the characteristic curved look. Cook for a couple of minutes, then turn on to a board and serve with a drizzle of extra virgin olive oil. It should still be lovely and juicy in the middle when you cut into it.

THE SPANISH HOME KITCHEN

CHERRY GAZPACHO

Many customers and friends are surprised when they learn that gazpacho can be made with such a variety of things, having always thought that gazpacho is just made with tomatoes. And yes, the classic tomato gazpacho is the most popular and well-known, but we love to get creative with it. Gazpacho is essentially a cold soup that can be smooth or textured, thin or thick – you can even get a 'partridge gazpacho' (a truly yummy recipe, but probably one for my next book!). In my book *Andalusia*, I gave a recipe for strawberry gazpacho, because in Huelva the fruit is great. Here, in this lovely book about my home and home cooking, I'm making it with cherries, because I grew up with some of the best cherries in the world. They are a remarkably high-quality product of Jerte, just north of my home village in Spain.

GAZPACHO

1 tablespoon olive oil
1 slice of stale white sourdough
2 garlic cloves, sliced
1 red (bell) pepper, deseeded
   and chopped
500 g (1 lb 2 oz) ripe red
   cherries, stoned
½ cucumber, peeled and diced
300 ml (10 fl oz/1¼ cups)
   tomato juice
2 tablespoons sherry vinegar
4 tablespoons extra virgin olive
   oil, plus 2 tablespoons to
   emulsify

TOPPINGS

2 tablespoons olive oil
1 thick slice of stale white
   sourdough, cut into
   small cubes
1 thyme sprig, leaves picked
½ small red onion,
   very finely chopped
50 g (2 oz) goat's cheese,
   crumbled
¼ cucumber, peeled and
   finely diced
handful of fresh basil leaves
extra virgin olive oil, for drizzling
sea salt and freshly ground
   black pepper

For the soup, heat the olive oil in a frying pan (skillet) over a medium-high heat and fry the bread on both sides until golden. Put into a bowl with the rest of the gazpacho ingredients (except for the 2 tablespoons of oil) and allow to sit for a couple of hours.

For the topping, heat a little of the oil in a frying pan over a medium-high heat. Add the cubes of bread and the thyme and fry until you have golden croutons. Drain on a plate lined with paper towels and season.

Blitz the soup really well with a hand-held blender, then push it through a coarse sieve (mesh strainer) into a jug (pitcher). Whisk in the 2 tablespoons extra virgin olive oil. Pour into 4 bowls and top with all the toppings, along with a drizzle of extra virgin olive oil.

TIP

You can can roast the peppers if you'd like the soup to have a softer flavour.

ZORONGOLLO

I came cross this wonderful recipe at my first job in Cáceres. Don't get me wrong, it was not my favourite dish to make at the time, because as the commis chef, it was my job to peel the peppers. I remember feeling frustrated, because all I wanted to do was to learn more and more, and all this peeling felt like a waste of time. However, I respected my head chef, Ana, and she always said, 'You must learn from the bottom, so get peeling!' Anyway, now I love to peel – and cook – either grilled or roasted peppers. The aroma they give off is just great: it's earthy and smoky, and really relaxes me. Of course, a bonus is that there are no pips at all – not one! As always, it's important to use a good-quality sherry vinegar and a really green extra virgin olive oil – these will help take this recipe to a different level.

My tip for you: this is arguably best done where the peppers and tomatoes can be cooked over hot coals on a barbecue to give a wonderful, charred flavour, but in the recipe below, I've given instructions for cooking it in the oven.

INGREDIENTS

3 very large red (bell) peppers
2 large vine tomatoes
3 garlic cloves, skin on
1 small red onion, finely sliced
olive oil, for drizzling
2 fresh thyme sprigs,
    leaves picked, plus extra
    to serve
2 tablespoons sherry vinegar
sea salt and freshly ground
    black pepper

TO SERVE

4 slices of toast, made with
    fresh crusty bread
2 hard-boiled free-range
    eggs, sliced
6–8 anchovies (optional)
1 tablespoon capers
    (baby capers)
2 teaspoons sherry vinegar
extra virgin olive oil, for drizzling

Preheat the oven to 220°C/200°C fan/425°F/gas 7. Arrange the peppers, tomatoes and garlic on a baking tray and drizzle all over with oil. Season well. Roast for 45 minutes until softened and well roasted.

Transfer into a bowl and cover with clingfilm (plastic wrap), then leave to cool. Once cool, remove all the skins, making sure you keep the juices for the marinade.

Put the tomato flesh and garlic in a pestle and mortar and crush. Tear the pepper flesh into long strips, discarding the core and seeds. Toss the tomatoes, garlic and peppers together with the juices, then add the onion and thyme and toss to combine. Add the sherry vinegar, then cover and leave to sit overnight in a cool place.

The next day, serve the *zorongollo* on fresh toast, topped with sliced hard-boiled eggs, torn anchovies and a scattering of capers. Drizzle with a little sherry vinegar and extra virgin olive oil, add a scattering of thyme leaves and enjoy.

FRESH COW'S CHEESE

Growing up on a farm, one of my great childhood memories is of my mum making fresh cheese every morning. She wouldn't make many cheeses – just one or two, depending on how many people we were in the house – because we all liked very fresh cheese. She would make it in the morning, and we'd normally finish it in the evening. The whole family loved it, but it was a particular favourite for my dad and my brother Antonio. We made the cheese with fresh milk from the best cows on the farm, the dried rennet from the stomach of a goat that my mum had in the cellar, and, of course, a really good dose of quality salt. Here is my version, which you can make at home. You can eat it super-fresh, or store it in brine for up to a month, but I'm sure it will be gone long before that. There are some ideas for how you can use this cheese on pages 66 and 160.

INGREDIENTS

5 litres (170 fl oz/5 quarts) raw full-fat (whole) milk or unhomogenised milk
5½ tablespoons vegetarian rennet (or normal rennet)
50 g (2 oz) sea salt

TO SERVE

extra-virgin olive oil, for drizzling
dried chilli (hot pepper) flakes
fresh thyme sprigs, leaves picked
toasted sourdough

Pour the milk into a wide-bottomed saucepan over a low heat and, using a cooking thermometer to measure the temperature, bring it up to 32–36°C (90–97°F). Stir in the rennet and set aside to settle for an hour.

After an hour, the mixture will have set like fromage frais or junket. Use a knife to cut it into 2.5-cm (1-in) cubes, which will release the whey (liquid) from the curds (solids). Leave to sit in the pan for another 30 minutes or so.

Return the pan to a low heat and gently bring up to 38°C (100°F). Scoop the curds into small moulds or ramekins lined with muslin (cheesecloth) set on wire racks over a roasting tin (pan). Reserve the whey. Once full, fold the muslin over the top of each mould and weight down. Leave to drain for at least 4 hours.

Remove the cheese from the pan and gently turn out from the moulds. Turn each piece over and return it to its mould, then wrap in muslin (cheesecloth) and weight again for a further 2 hours.

Make a brine by mixing 500 ml (17 fl oz/2 cups) of the whey with 500 ml (17 fl oz/2 cups) water and 50 g (2 oz) salt. Once the salt has dissolved, you can slide your cheese into this brine and store for a week or so in the fridge. The cheese will be ready to eat once it has been in the brine for a few hours.

Put on a serving plate and drizzle with oil and scatter over chilli flakes and thyme leaves. Serve with toasted sourdough.

MUSHROOMS ON TOAST WITH TORTA DEL CASAR CHEESE

There are people who love cheese and people who hate cheese. Personally, I love cheese so much I could live on it! Well, I'd need some sherry too, but we all have to drink to survive, right? So, of the cheeses I really love, Torta del Casar is one of my favourites – I think it's one of the best cheeses in the world. It is made from sheep's milk, and has a silky, creamy texture, along with a bold aroma and a rich, slightly salty, flavour. There is a subtle bitterness to it that balances so well with the ripe creaminess. Cutting off the top of this cheese to reveal the creaminess within is a magical experience: it is like fondue at room temperature! Follow this recipe to heaven on a plate. As you can see in the picture, it is more cheese than mushrooms. Divine.

INGREDIENTS

8 small slices of crusty
　white bread
3 tablespoons olive oil
400 g (14 oz) mixed
　mushrooms, torn
2 garlic cloves, finely sliced
5 thyme sprigs, leaves picked
140 g (5 oz) Torta del Casar
　cheese, at room temperature
sea salt flakes
　thyme sprigs, to garnish

Heat a frying pan over a medium–high heat. Drizzle the bread with some of the oil on both sides and fry in the pan until golden, working in batches if necessary, then set aside and sprinkle with a little flaky sea salt.

Return the empty pan to the heat, increasing the heat a little. Add the remaining oil and, once hot, add the mushrooms. Cook for 3–4 minutes until lightly golden, then add the garlic and thyme leaves. Cook for a further 2 minutes until everything is golden and caramelised.

Spoon the mushrooms over the toast slices, scatter with thyme sprigs, then spoon over the gooey Torta del Casar and serve.

TIP

Torta del Casar needs to be really ripe for it to be spoonable. If it's not as gooey as you would like, dollop spoonfuls on to the toasts and then pop under a hot grill (broiler) for 10–20 seconds to melt the cheese a little.

RAW PUMPKIN SALAD WITH CANDIED CHESTNUTS

Autumn is one of my favourite seasons. Whenever I travel to the Basque country or Galicia at this time of year, I notice how similar the colour schemes are to those in the UK, maybe because they share a similar tree profile. All those coppery colours and crisp, fresh days when the sun is lower in the sky can feel very romantic, and this dish really captures that feeling for me. Of course, back in Extremadura, pumpkin is traditionally cooked in stews or soups, but serving it raw is just heaven for me. The particular combination of flavours in this recipe warms the soul, and is very special.

CANDIED CHESTNUTS

olive oil, for greasing
100 g (3½ oz/scant ½ cup) caster (superine) sugar
2 tablespoons water
150 g (5 oz) Fire-roasted Chestnuts (page 46), peeled and quartered

SALAD

½ large Delica pumpkin, thinly sliced using a mandolin or vegetable peeler
120 ml (4 fl oz/½ cup) apple cider vinegar
50 ml (1¾ fl oz/3 tablespoons) water
50 g (2 oz/scant ¼ cup) caster (superfine) sugar
1 teaspoon fennel seeds
3 tablespoons extra virgin olive oil
¼ frisée lettuce, leaves separated
100 g (3½ oz) curd cheese, crumbled
seeds of 1 pomegranate
sea salt and freshly ground black pepper

Begin by preparing the candied chestnuts. Grease a baking tray with olive oil, then put the sugar and water into a small saucepan over a low heat. Heat gently until all the sugar has dissolved; this will take around 5 minutes. Now increase the heat to medium and cook until you have golden/amber coloured caramel, swirling the pan from time to time to stop it from catching. Add the chestnuts and stir to coat, then pour this mixture on to the baking tray. Allow to cool.

Place the pumpkin slices in a bowl. Put the apple cider vinegar, water, sugar and fennel seeds into a small clean saucepan over a low heat. Heat for 5 minutes until the sugar has dissolved and the mixture comes to a boil. Bubble for a minute or two, then pour the mixture over the prepared pumpkin and leave for 45 minutes.

Taste the pumpkin to test it is sharp enough for your liking: it should have a good bite. Strain the pumpkin, reserving the pickling liquor. In a small jug (pitcher) or bowl, whisk 100 ml (3½ fl oz/scant ½ cup) of the pickle liquid with the extra virgin olive oil to make a dressing. Season to taste. In a large salad bowl, toss together the lettuce leaves and marinated pumpkin, then scatter the cheese over top. Break apart the candied chestnuts and scatter over the top, along with the pomegranate seeds. Drizzle with the dressing and finish with a good sprinkle of freshly ground black pepper.

FIRE-ROASTED CHESTNUTS

There's something remarkable about the way certain dishes trigger vivid memories: of people, places, certain times of the year, smells, flavours, conversations … they can bring back all the details of experiences we thought we'd forgotten. Roasted chestnuts are one of the foods that do this for me – they transport me back in time! They take me to a time when my dear friend Elsa and I (we were an inseparable, dynamic duo) were roasting and peeling chestnuts out in the countryside, tucking in to them as we went. This is colloquially known as *carboteo* –roasting chestnuts over an open fire outdoors, either on skewers or in a pan. Such precious memories.

Halloween was not recognised or celebrated in my village when I was a kid, but I think it has become a more of a thing more recently. It's still not a festival that I get particularly excited about, but I know many people do, and I do love that time of the year. There's something magical about the feeling you get when the air gets cooler, the leaves start falling from the trees, and you see chestnuts arriving in the local stores. I often use chestnuts in the restaurant (when they're in season) because they give a unique, hearty flavour, which is perfect for adding to numerous dishes – and by the way, they're absolutely stunning in stews.

INGREDIENTS

400 g (14 oz) chestnuts, each with a cross cut into the base or pierced with a skewer

Heat a fire or barbecue until just red-hot coals remain.

Place a chestnut roaster or a heavy cast-iron pan in the centre of the coals, then add the chestnuts. Cook for 15–20 minutes, or until the outside is slightly charred and the skin is starting to peel open.

PUMPKIN, AUBERGINE AND PEPPER STEW

I have to admit, I was not a very good student – not good at all. I preferred to be out and about, running freely around my village, Talaván, with my friends rather than sitting in front of books. The problem with this approach is that if you don't do your homework, you don't pass your exams! That happened to me often, and my family call that 'bringing pumpkin to the house'. My mum would say: *'¡José! ¿Cuantas calabazas?!'* Well, it was enough pumpkin for the whole year, I'm telling you! I'm not proud of that, but it's how I was.

This gorgeous recipe is a stew I just love. It's not dissimilar to the pisto recipe that you may know from my book *Spanish Flavours,* but this one has a rich autumnal tone thanks to the pumpkin and chickpeas. For the vinegar, I suggest you use just 2 teaspoons to begin with (personally, I love more – just be careful with it!).

INGREDIENTS

4 tablespoons olive oil
1 large onion, finely chopped
2 garlic cloves, grated
1 large aubergine (eggplant), chopped
½ teaspoon dried chilli (hot pepper) flakes
½ teaspoon bittersweet pimentón de la Vera
3 marjoram or oregano sprigs
1 green (bell) pepper, chopped
2 red (bell) peppers, chopped
800 g (1 lb 12 oz) peeled and chopped pumpkin or squash
400 g (14 oz) tin chopped tomatoes
400 ml (13 fl oz/generous 1½ cups) vegetable stock
1 bay leaf
400 g (14 oz) tin chickpeas (garbanzos), drained and rinsed
2 teaspoons sherry vinegar
extra virgin olive oil, for drizzling
large handful of flat-leaf parsley, stalks and leaves chopped
sea salt and freshly ground black pepper

Heat the oil in a large casserole dish (Dutch oven) or sauté pan over a low heat. Add the onion, garlic and aubergine (eggplant) and gently fry for 15 minutes. Add the chilli (hot pepper) flakes, pimentón and marjoram or oregano and fry for a minute more, then add the peppers and pumpkin. Increase the heat a little and cook for another 10 minutes.

Add the tomatoes, stock, bay leaf and parsley stalks. Season well and reduce the heat to low. Simmer for 40 minutes until the veggies are very tender and have formed a lovely thick stew.

Add the chickpeas (garbanzos) and vinegar and bubble for 10 minutes or so, then serve with a drizzle of extra virgin olive oil and a scattering of chopped parsley leaves.

CREAMY MILK AND ROAST GARLIC SOUP

WITH MANCHEGO AND GREEN OLIVE TOAST

In Spain, garlic is the king of the herbs, and it's very important in our cooking. So, this recipe is all about the garlic – turn the page if you're not a fan!

There is truly nothing like this soup. If you've never tried it, stop what you're doing and make it now! It's a favourite recipe of my mum's, although her version is much simpler: she just fries the garlic, sometimes with a little jamón, then adds a bay leaf, a bit of water and milk, some salt and the bread. She brings it to the boil – and it's ready. She has an amazing gift for bringing out fantastic flavours with just a few simple but great ingredients.

Here, I've developed the dish a little further, adding a bit of my chef's touch, but still honouring the essence of it.

INGREDIENTS

3 tablespoons olive oil
2 garlic bulbs
100 g (3½ oz) fresh white
  breadcrumbs
1 teaspoon pimentón de la Vera
1 litre (34 fl oz/4 cups) fresh
  vegetable stock
200 ml (7 fl oz/scant 1 cup)
  full-fat (whole) milk
sea salt and freshly ground
  black pepper

GREEN OLIVE TOAST

200 g (7 oz) pitted green olives,
  roughly chopped
2 tablespoons capers
  (baby capers)
1 garlic clove
finely grated zest of ½ lemon,
  plus a good squeeze of juice
4 tablespoons extra virgin
  olive oil
6 slices of crusty bread
olive oil, for drizzling
75 g (2½ oz) Manchego, grated

Preheat the oven to 180°C/160°C fan/350°F/gas 4. Rub 1 tablespoon of the oil all over the garlic bulbs and place them in a small roasting tin (pan). Cook for 20–30 minutes until tender. Allow to cool, then squeeze out the soft garlic cloves into a bowl and mash with a fork. Leave the oven on a for a later step.

Heat the remaining oil in a frying pan (skillet) over a medium-high heat and fry the breadcrumbs for 4–5 minutes until golden. Tip into a saucepan over a medium-high heat. Add the mashed garlic and pimentón and season well, then fry for another minute. Pour in the stock and bring to a simmer. Bubble for 20 minutes, then blitz with a hand-held blender until smooth.

Meanwhile, make the olive toast. Put the olives, capers and garlic into a small food processor and pulse to form a rough paste. Whizz in the lemon zest and juice and extra virgin olive oil. Season to taste.

Arrange the sliced of bread on a baking sheet and drizzle with oil. Place in the oven and toast lightly on both sides for 2 minutes.

Spread each slice of toast with the green olive mixture and scatter over the cheese. Return to the oven and cook for a further 2–3 minutes until the cheese has melted.

Add the milk to the soup and bubble for a few minutes, then pour into bowls. Float a piece of toast in each and serve.

THE SPANISH HOME KITCHEN

CARAJAMANDANGA

OK, so the name of this recipe really makes me laugh. I have no idea where the name came from, as it doesn't make any sense in Spanish. You have to move all the muscles in your mouth and tongue to pronounce it! If you ask people what this recipe is, or try to look it up, you'll find many different explanations. In my humble opinion, it is essentially a member of the gazpacho family. Normally, you would chop all the ingredients together, but here I suggest making a smooth mixture with some of the ingredients as a dressing for the rest – it's just delicious. Perfect for a hot day, or just whenever you're in the mood – why not?

INGREDIENTS

100 g (3½ oz) stale white bread, torn
600 ml (20 fl oz/2½ cups) water
2 garlic cloves
800 g (1 lb 12 oz) tomatoes, chopped
2 teaspoons bittersweet pimentón de la Vera
1 tablespoon apple vinegar
1 red (bell) pepper, chopped
1 courgette (zucchini), chopped
½ cucumber, peeled, deseeded and chopped
120 g (4 oz) pitted black olives, roughly chopped
2 tablespoons snipped chives
extra virgin olive oil, for drizzling
sea salt and freshly ground black pepper

Put the bread, water and garlic in a food processor and whizz together to form a smooth mixture with about the consistency of single (light) cream. Add two thirds of the tomatoes, along with the pimentón and vinegar. Season well and whizz again until smooth. You can add a splash of water if it's a little too thick.

Pour the mixture into a large bowl and add the remaining tomatoes. Reserve a couple of spoons of the pepper, courgette (zucchini) and cucumber for the garnish, then add the rest to the bowl. Check the seasoning, then chill for at least 3 hours.

To serve, scatter with the olives, vegetable garnish and chives and drizzle with extra virgin olive oil. Season with plenty of freshly ground black pepper and enjoy.

TIP

You can can roast the peppers if you'd like the soup to have a softer flavour.

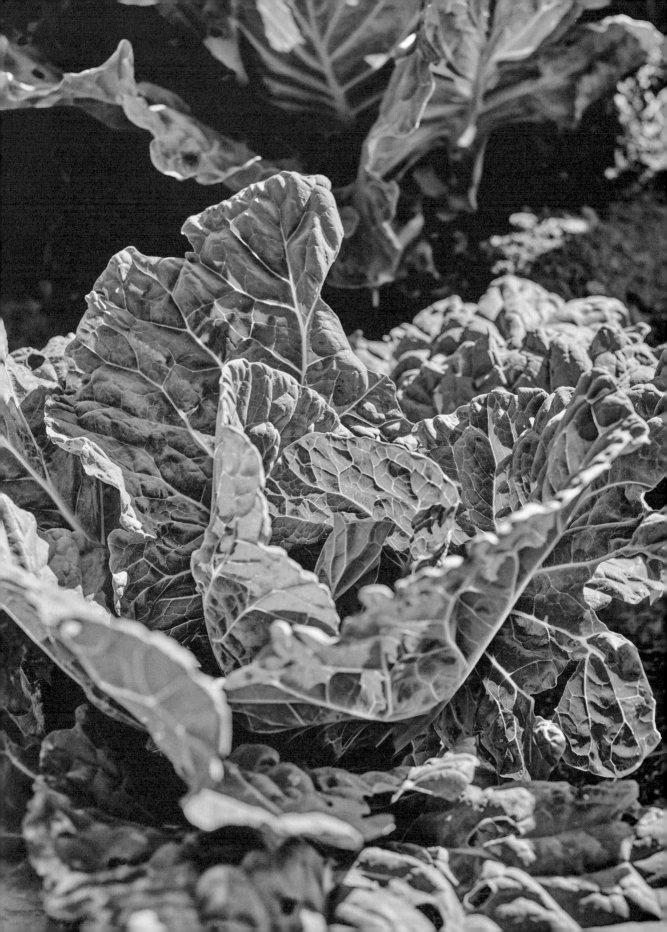

TOMATO, BEETROOT, WHITE BEAN AND POMEGRANATE SALAD

When people ask if I enjoy cooking at home, I tell them the truth: I love it. It really relaxes me after work. As I'm sure you can understand, after a long shift in a restaurant, you wouldn't want to cook a complex three-course meal. But something straightforward that will make you feel good? Absolutely. It's like painting for artists, or writing for writers: cooking is a creative process. You can explore the cupboards and fridge to see what ingredients you can find, then use your imagination to create something delicious. It's always good to have few different tins of things like beans and pulses in the pantry. A salad like this will always be my go-to – it's easy to make, and enjoyable to eat!

INGREDIENTS

2 beetroots (beets)
1 teaspoon olive oil
400 g (14 oz) tin white beans, such as butter (lima) beans, drained and rinsed
700 g (1 lb 9 oz) heritage tomatoes, roughly chopped
seeds from 1 pomegranate

THYME DRESSING

1½ tablespoons sherry vinegar
2 fresh thyme sprigs, leaves picked, with flowers if you can
1½ tablespoons pomegranate molasses
3–4 tablespoons extra virgin olive oil

TO SERVE (OPTIONAL)

Manchego
rocket (arugula) leaves
crusty bread

Preheat the oven to 200°C/180°C fan/400°F/gas 6. Rub the beetroots (beets) with the oil and wrap each one in kitchen foil. Roast for 45 minutes until tender. Allow to cool until they are cool enough to handle, then peel and chop.

Toss the white beans with the beetroots, tomatoes, and pomegranate seeds to the bowl and toss together.

Make the dressing, blend the sherry vinegar, thyme and pomegranate molasses together then gradually whisk in the extra virgin olive oil. Drizzle all over the still warm salad and toss together.

Let it sit for 10 minutes then serve with Manchego, rocket (arugula) and crusty bread.

SAUTÉED JERUSALEM ARTICHOKES WITH JAMÓN IBÉRICO AND KALE

In 2001, something happened that changed my whole relationship with food and cooking: I started working at Eyre Brothers restaurant with David and Rob Eyre. I always loved David's pub The Eagle (and still do), and it was extremely humbling to be asked to be his sous-chef at his new venture. Within a few months, I was running his kitchen, but I was also learning – and getting back to my roots. I'd been cooking Michelin-star type food for many years, but at Eyre Brothers, I learned to cook sincerely from my heart, using one of the most important ingredients for me: 'memories'. Memories of my moments with family and friends, and memories of different times in my life.

This is a recipe from the time I spent at Eyre Brothers, and I still remember the first time I cooked it. It was David's dish – I used it as a garnish for hake, and it's just great. I cook this one sometimes at home, and one of my favourite twists on it is to add a couple of fried eggs – crispy around the outside, of course, in true Spanish style.

INGREDIENTS

250 ml (8½ fl oz/1 cup) olive oil
600 g (1 lb 5 oz) Jerusalem artichokes, scrubbed and sliced into 3-mm (⅛-in) rounds
4 garlic cloves, sliced
3 thyme sprigs, leaves stripped
100 g (3½ oz) jamón ibérico
200 g (7 oz) kale, finely shredded
1 teaspoon sherry vinegar
extra virgin olive oil, for drizzling
2 tablespoons finely chopped chives
sea salt and freshly ground black pepper

Heat the oil in a deep sauté pan over a medium heat. Once quite hot, add the artichokes and cook gently for 8–10 minutes, adding the garlic cloves for the last 2 minutes.

Scoop the garlic and artichokes out of the pan with a slotted spoon and set aside on a plate lined with paper towels. Drain off almost all of the oil. Return the artichokes and garlic to the pan, along with the thyme and jamón, and increase the heat to high. Cook for 10–15 minutes until the artichokes and jamón are golden. Scoop out and set aside on a plate, and season with salt and pepper.

Now add the kale to the pan, along with a splash of water, and cook for a few minutes to wilt.

To serve, divide the kale between 4–6 plates, then spoon the artichokes and jamón on top. Drizzle with the vinegar and some extra virgin olive oil, then scatter over the chives and serve.

GIROLLE AND WALNUT CROQUETAS

In my dad's vegetable garden, we have the most elegant and stunning walnut tree that produces walnuts for us all year round. Walnuts were a type of candy for me when I was little. I would wait for them to be ready, watching as the tiny fruits emerged before summer, eager to be able to crack them open and eat the first ones. Walnuts really stain your hands when you open them, so unfortunately my dad always knew I was eating them – it was very difficult to hide the evidence! These delicious vegan croquetas are one of my all-time favourites, and great for a special occasion. The secret to any good croquetas is to make them with decent bechamel. This one is a real winner at parties – and remember, you can freeze them. Take them out of the freezer about thirty minutes before you need them, they'll be ready to fry.

INGREDIENTS

15 g (½ oz) dried wild mushrooms
125 ml (4¼ fl oz/½ cup) boiling water
150 ml (5 fl oz/scant ⅔ cup) olive oil
2 garlic cloves, grated
250 g (9 oz) fresh girolles
125 g (4 oz/1 cup) plain (all-purpose) flour
500 ml (17 fl oz/2 cups) fresh vegetable stock, warm
1 tablespoon finely chopped tarragon
50 g (2 oz/scant ½ cup) walnuts, chopped
1 litre (34 fl oz/4 cups) vegetable oil, for deep-frying
sea salt and freshly ground black pepper

COATING

3 tablespoons plain (all-purpose) flour
25 g (½ oz/scant ¼ cup) walnuts, chopped
4 tablespoons olive oil
150 g (5 oz/1¼ cups) panko breadcrumbs

Place the dried mushrooms in a bowl with the boiling water and leave to soak for 10 minutes. Drain, reserving the soaking liquor.

Heat 50 ml (1¾ fl oz/3 tablespoons) of the olive oil in a frying pan over a high heat. Add the garlic and fry for 30 seconds, then add the drained mushrooms and the girolles and fry for 10 minutes until golden. Season well.

In a separate saucepan, heat the rest of the oil over a high heat. Add the flour and cook for 2–3 minutes, then gradually add the warm stock, stirring, until you have a smooth, very thick bechamel. Add the mushroom soaking liquor and stir, then season. Roughly chop the mushrooms and add them to the bechamel with the tarragon and walnuts.

Spread the mixture out on a baking sheet lined with clingfilm (plastic wrap), cover and chill until cold.

Once cold, take spoonfuls of the mixture and roll into 30 balls of about 30 g (1 oz) each.

To coat the *croquetas*, blitz the flour and walnuts together in a small food processor, then transfer this mixture to a dish. Pour the olive oil into a second dish and the breadcrumbs into a third.

Coat each of the balls in walnut flour, then olive oil, then breadcrumbs, then place on a baking sheet. When they are all coated, freeze for 1 hour.

When you're ready to cook, pour the oil for deep-frying into a saucepan over a high heat. Heat the oil to 180°C/350°F, or until a cube of bread browns in around 30 seconds. Drop a few of the *croquetas* into the oil and fry for 3–4 minutes until deep golden and hot to the centre. Remove with a slotted spoon and set aside on a plate lined with paper towels while you fry the rest. Serve straight away.

WARM GLOBE ARTICHOKE SALAD

WITH HOMEMADE CHEESE, PINE NUTS AND CARAMELISED LEMON DRESSING

This salad combines some of my favourite flavours. I have a longstanding love of artichokes, and cooking them with jamón Ibérico lardons takes them to the next level thanks to the gorgeous nutty flavours that come from the fat – just sublime. The lemon makes a perfect addition, cutting through the richness of the lardons, while the pine nuts add a delicious crunch.

Pine nuts are very important in my cooking, and I've loved them since I was a kid. We used to go and gather pinecones in the hills of Talaván on very cold winter mornings. The gorgeous aroma coming from the resin was something very special. We'd keep the pinecones until summer and then lay them out under the sun to open, cracking the outer shells to get to the pine nuts inside.

INGREDIENTS

6 globe artichokes
juice of 1 lemon
2–3 tablespoons olive oil,
    plus extra for drizzling
100 g (3½ oz) jamón ibérico
    lardons (or bacon or pancetta
    lardons)
bunch of spring onions
    (scallions)
500 g (1 lb 2 oz) fresh peas,
    shelled
150 g (5 oz) Fresh Cow's Cheese
    (page 38), crumbled, or feta or
    crumbly goat's cheese
50 g (2 oz/⅓ cup) pine nuts,
    toasted

Trim the globe artichoke stems and cut 2–3 cm (1-1½ in) off the top of the leaves. Pull off the tough outer leaves. When you get to the soft inner leaves, halve the artichokes lengthways, then hollow out and remove the choke and fibres from above the heart. Place the artichokes in a bowl of water with the lemon juice as you go to prevent browning.

Bring a pan of water to the boil, then simmer the artichokes for 10–12 minutes until tender. Drain and allow to cool to room temperature.

Heat the oil in a frying pan over a medium-high heat. Add the lardons and fry for 6–8 minutes until golden. Scoop them out of the pan with a slotted spoon and tip into a serving bowl, along with the cooled artichokes.

Add the spring onions (scallions) to the pan. Increase the heat and sear for 2-3 minutes until golden, then add to the dish.

To make the dressing, heat the sugar and water in a small saucepan over a medium heat until the sugar dissolves. Bring to the boil and bubble until just turning golden, then add the lemon slices and stir until coated and caramelised, around 5–10 minutes. Transfer to a bowl.

DRESSING

50 g (2 oz/scant ¼ cup)
    caster (superfine) sugar
2 tablespoons water
1 lemon, thinly sliced
2 teaspoons Dijon mustard
2 teaspoons apple cider vinegar
3–4 tablespoons extra virgin
    olive oil
sea salt
freshly ground black pepper

In a small bowl, whisk the mustard with the vinegar. Season with salt and pepper, then whisk in the extra virgin olive oil. Add this to the caramelised lemon slices.

Cook the peas in boiling water for a couple of minutes, then cool under running water. Add to the serving dish, along with the crumbled cheese and toasted pine nuts. Pour over the dressing, toss to combine and serve.

THE SPANISH HOME KITCHEN

ESCALIVADA SALAD WITH ROASTED TOMATO DRESSING

I think I have an escalivada salad in almost every book I've ever written, because I love it so much and it's a dish you can be really creative with. All of my escalivada recipes are different, but share one very important common element: roasted vegetables! However you make it, it's always a winner. For this recipe, I've changed things slightly by blending the roasted tomatoes with the juices from the other roasted vegetables, along with a dash of vinegar. It makes a superb dressing that is perfect with this warm, tasty salad. Enjoy!

INGREDIENTS

2 aubergines (eggplants), sliced
2 red (bell) peppers
1 yellow (bell) pepper
2 red onions, cut into wedges
3 vine tomatoes, halved
1 garlic bulb, cloves separated
4 thyme sprigs, leaves picked
75 ml (2½ fl oz/5 tablespoons) olive oil, plus 2 tablespoons extra to fry
2 teaspoons pimentón de la Vera
2 teaspoons sherry vinegar
4 tablespoons extra virgin olive oil
100 g (3½ oz) stale bread, torn
1 tablespoon capers
50 g (2 oz) Manchego, shaved
sea salt and freshly ground black pepper

Preheat the oven to 220°C/200°C fan/425°F/gas 7. Put the aubergine (eggplant), peppers, onion wedges, tomatoes, garlic and thyme on a large baking sheet. Drizzle with the oil and sprinkle with the pimentón. Toss to coat well. Roast for 20 minutes, then remove the garlic and set aside. Continue to roast the other vegetables for a further 20–30 minutes until the pepper skins are blackened and the rest of the vegetables are sticky and tender.

Put the peppers in a dish and cover with clingfilm (plastic wrap). Leave to stand for 10 minutes, or until cool enough to handle, then remove the skins and seeds and thinly slice the flesh. Save any juices to add to the dressing.

To make the roasted tomato dressing, put the roasted tomatoes in a blender with the vinegar and extra virgin olive oil. Season well and blitz, adding any juices from the peppers and a splash of water until you have a dressing-like consistency.

Heat the 2 tablespoons olive oil in a frying pan over a medium-high heat. Add the torn bread and fry for 5–10 minutes until golden. Drain on a plate lined with paper towels and season with sea salt.

Toss all the veggies in a dish with the capers, Manchego, croutons, reserved garlic and dressing, and serve it straight away.

FISH AND SEAFOOD

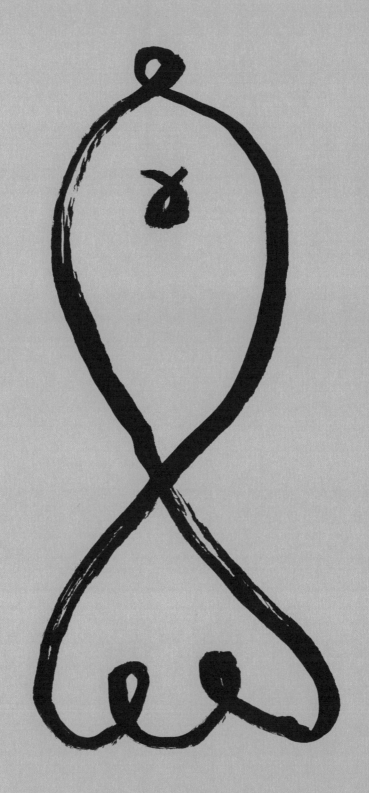

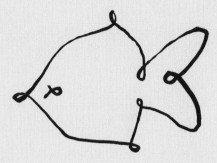

Memories of fishing with my dad are forever etched in my mind. My village in rural Spain is located near a long, beautiful winding river called the Tajo, and we would often fish there together. It only takes about twenty minutes to walk to the river from the heart of the village, and it's a fantastic walk, especially in the springtime, when all the flowers are in bloom. The river is generally wide, extremely deep in places, and its movement is mesmerising.

Every village in Spain has a Virgin Patróna who watches over things. Ours is 'La Virgen del Río' (Virgin of the River). Traditionally, all the villagers walk together along the old country lanes that lead to the river on the first sunday in May each year for the Fiesta del Virgin (any excuse!) – it's a very beautiful and special place.

From the chapel, the views of the waters and surrounding landscape are spectacular. Water levels normally drop in the summer and stay that way until late autumn when the rain returns, but it's still possible to fish. Back in the day, my dad and I would fish all year round because the fish were plentiful and there were no restrictions or limitations. We'd catch a small, tasty local freshwater fish called tenca. There's an annual fiesta for the tenca, held in one or another of the local villages. One year, I was awarded the Tenca d'Oro – the Golden Tenca – in honour of my work raising the profile of Extremadura and all its wonderful produce. Another fish we'd catch regularly is called black bass. The dialect is strong where I come from, the equivalent of a thick Scottish accent here in the UK, so the people call the fish 'blas blas', which sounds more like 'blah blah' when you hear it. I don't know why, but this always makes me smile.

I've been lucky enough to fish at sea, too, and I've had some brilliant experiences on fishing boats. Not so long ago, I went on a fishing excursion to Norway, where we fished for skrei. The seawater there is extremely cold, and the fish have battled with strong currents, making them big, strong, and meaty. The water is crystal-clear, and when you catch the fish, you see them as things of real beauty. People are particularly ecologically conscious in Norway and aware of the need to maintain fish levels appropriately, and I liked this respect for the sea. It's so important to know what's behind any of the produce we eat, and I am a big advocate of responsible fishing. As with meat, when I'm cooking at home or in the restaurant, I always want to know where the fish has come from and how it's been caught.

PICKLED OYSTERS

When King Carlos V retired to the monastery of Yuste in 1556, he made sure he continued to have access to the rarest and most incredible foods available. One of the great delicacies of the time was fresh oysters (although they probably weren't so good for his gout). Although Yuste is a beautiful area, it is very remote. I can only imagine how difficult it would have been to transport oysters there, and I wonder what kind of preserving methods might have been used. These gorgeous pickled oysters are a wonderful way of enhancing those fresh sea flavours, and they're a firm favourite in my home. Pickled oysters all the way!

INGREDIENTS

1 small shallot, very finely sliced
2 teaspoons very finely
   chopped carrot
1 teaspoon very finely
   chopped celery
125 ml (4¼ fl oz/½ cup)
   Moscatel vinegar
125 ml (4¼ fl oz/½ cup) water
½ teaspoon coriander seeds
1 small fresh bay leaf
1 teaspoon sea salt
2 teaspoons honey
½ teaspoon sweet smoked
   pimentón de la Vera
12 rock oysters, shucked
   (but keep the half-shell)
extra virgin olive oil, for drizzling

Put the vegetables in a small saucepan with the vinegar, water, coriander seeds, bay leaf, salt, honey and pimentón. Bring to a simmer over a low heat and cook for 2–4 minutes.

Put the shucked oysters in a ceramic bowl and pour the hot pickle liquid over the top to cover completely. Leave to stand for 10 minutes. You can then chill for up to 24 hours until you are ready to serve.

To serve, place an oyster and a little of the pickle into each half-shell and arrange on a platter. Drizzle with extra virgin olive oil and enjoy.

THE SPANISH HOME KITCHEN

HAKE CROQUETAS

Do you like croquetas? Maybe it's a stupid question – doesn't everyone? When they're made well, I think these are the best croquetas in the world – and, of course, this recipe is from my mum. The hake recipe on page 85 is more or less the same as here, but without the salsa (although you could make the salsa and use it as a dip, if you like). Once you've battered the croquetas, you can freeze them – just take them out 30 minutes before you want to fry them. My mum always has croquetas in the freezer for when I pay her a surprise visit! Always prepared. I know you will love this recipe.

INGREDIENTS

2 tablespoons olive oil
1 large onion, finely sliced
1 bay leaf
200 ml (7 fl oz/scant 1 cup) white wine
300 g (10½ oz) fresh hake fillet
3 tablespoons plain (all-purpose) flour
1 large free-range egg, beaten
125 g (4 oz/generous 2 cups) panko breadcrumbs
1.2 litres (40 fl oz/4¾ cups) vegetable or olive oil

BECHAMEL

75 ml (2½ fl oz/5 tablespoons) olive oil
75 g (2½ oz/scant ⅔ cup) plain (all-purpose) flour
250 ml (8½ fl oz/1 cup) full-fat (whole) milk
sea salt and freshly ground black pepper

TO SERVE

alioli (page 88)

Heat the oil in a frying pan over a low heat and gently fry the onion with the bay leaf for 15 minutes until really lovely and soft. Add the white wine and hake to the pan, then increase the heat and bring to a simmer. Cover and cook for 10 minutes.

Scoop out the hake and onion with a slotted spoon. Reserve 150 ml (5 fl oz/scant ⅔ cup) of the cooking juices and set aside, discarding the bay leaf.

Place the hake and onion in a food processor and whizz to combine.

To make the bechamel sauce, heat the oil in a saucepan over a medium heat and add the flour. Cook for a couple of minutes, then gradually add the reserved cooking juices, followed by the milk, stirring continuously until you have a very thick, smooth sauce. Season well, then stir in the whizzed hake and onions. Mix together, then spoon into a dish and chill for at least 2 hours.

Once chilled, take spoonfuls of the mixture (abut 30 g/ 1 oz each) and shape each one into an oval.

Put the flour in one shallow dish, the egg in a second and the breadcrumbs in a third. Dust each *croqueta* with flour, then coat in egg and finally in crumbs. Place them on a baking sheet and chill until ready to cook (you can also freeze them at this point).

Pour the oil into a large, deep saucepan and heat to 180°C (350°F), or until a cube of bread browns in 30 seconds. Fry the *croquetas* a few at a time, cooking them for 2–3 minutes until golden brown and piping hot. Scoop out with a slotted spoon and set aside on a plate lined with paper towels. Sprinkle with sea salt and repeat with the remaining croquettes then serve with the alioli.

FRIED SARDINES

WITH WARM LENTIL SALAD, FENNEL AND A LEMON SALSA VERDE

This recipe has come a very long way with me: I've been making it since I was working at Eyre Brothers. I don't play around with it much, because it really works just as it is. Sometimes I make it with anchovies, but here, I'm doing it without. The first time I saw salsa verde being made this way, I was a bit baffled, because in most parts of Spain, a salsa verde is actually a very light white sauce: it's very popular in the Basque country, where they make a gorgeous dish involving hake, white asparagus, clams, peas and plenty of parsley. This zesty green version pairs perfectly with the fried sardines and earthy lentils.

INGREDIENTS

2 tablespoons olive oil
1 banana shallot, finely sliced
1 garlic clove, finely sliced
200 g (7 oz/1¼ cups) puy lentils
1 bay leaf
500 ml (17 fl oz/2 cups)
  vegetable stock
8 sardines, butterflied
2 tablespoons white wine
  vinegar
125 ml (4¼ fl oz/½ cup) white
  wine
8 black peppercorns
1 teaspoon coriander seeds
good pinch of caster
  (superfine) sugar
1 red onion, finely sliced
1 large fennel bulb, very finely
  sliced with a mandolin
sea salt and freshly ground
  black pepper

SALSA VERDE

30 g (1 oz) flat-leaf parsley,
  finely chopped
10 g (½ oz) fennel fronds,
  finely chopped
1 tablespoon capers
  (baby capers)
½ green chilli, finely chopped
  (optional)
zest and juice of 1 lemon
90 ml (3 fl oz/⅓ cup) extra virgin
  olive oil

Heat half the oil in a saucepan over a low heat and gently fry the shallot and garlic for 5 minutes. Add the lentils, bay leaf and stock, and season well. Increase the heat and bring to a boil, then reduce the heat to low and simmer for 15 minutes until the lentils are just tender. Drain well and tip on to a serving platter.

In a small saucepan over a medium-high heat, mix together the vinegar, white wine, peppercorns, coriander seeds and sugar. Reduce by half, then toss with the red onion in a small bowl.

In another small bowl, mix together all the salsa ingredients and season well.

Heat the rest of the oil in a non-stick frying pan (skillet) over a high heat and fry the sardine fillets, skin-side down, for 2 minutes until crisp and golden. Flip over and fry for another minute until just cooked. Remove from the heat and set aside.

Toss the finely shredded fennel with the lentils. Top with the sardines and scatter over the pickled red onion, then drizzle with the salsa verde.

PAN-FRIED HALIBUT

WITH SMOKED PIMENTÓN OIL AND A CHORICERO CABBAGE SALAD

I adore pan-fried halibut, and here I've put together the perfect accompaniment. I based it on a side dish that is really popular in Talaván. It's more than a salad – it's almost like a gazpacho. We don't cook the cabbage, just shred it really finely, then use a mortar and pestle to bring together the garlic, the choricero, some good-quality vinegar and plenty of extra virgin olive oil. This is added to the cabbage, which is then covered with water. The result is so simple, but the flavours are truly divine, and remind me of being at home with my mum and dad.

CHORICERO CABBAGE SALAD

1 sweetheart (pointed) cabbage, very finely shredded
1 dried choricero chilli
2–3 tablespoons olive oil
2 garlic cloves, finely sliced
50 g (2 oz) stale bread, torn
yolk from 1 hardboiled egg, mashed
60 ml (2 fl oz/¼ cup) water
sea salt and freshly ground black pepper

HALIBUT

4 halibut steaks on the bone (200–250 g/7–9 oz each)
2 tablespoons extra virgin olive oil
1 teaspoon hot smoked pimentón de la Vera flakes
2 teaspoons sherry vinegar
pared zest of 1 lemon

Begin by making the cabbage salad. Put the cabbage in a large bowl. Rehydrate the choricero in boiling water for 15 minutes. Heat the oil in a frying pan (skillet) over a medium heat and fry the garlic and bread for 5 minutes until golden.

Put the choricero and its soaking water in a small food processor. Add the fried garlicky bread and blitz to combine. Season, then add the egg yolk and water and whizz until you have a smooth dressing. Pour this over the cabbage and toss well, then set aside.

For the fish, heat a large frying pan (skillet) over a high heat. Brush the fish with some of the oil and fry on the first side for 2–3 minutes.

Meanwhile, heat the rest of the oil in a small pan over a medium-high heat. Add the pimentón flakes, vinegar and lemon zest and stir to combine, cooking for 3–4 minutes. Set aside.

Turn the fish over and cook for 2–3 minutes on the other side, then pour over the flavoured oil, letting it sizzle. Serve the pan-fried fish with the cabbage.

FRIED SALT COD AND EGG STEW

Spain, in particular Castilla la Mancha, produces one of the best saffrons in the world. I have been lucky enough to be there and collect the flowers in the morning and then pick the threads to be dried. I have to say it was a very relaxing day, and at the end I realised why the saffron is the most expensive spice in the world, with everything being done so carefully by hand. The good thing is you don't need too much of it to really make a difference to a dish; the flavour is so characterful and of course it's a lovely colour, too. This is another favourite recipe from back home that's often served on Easter Friday. Isabel doesn't use saffron in her version, but for me it works perfectly.

INGREDIENTS

5 free-range eggs
500 ml (17 fl oz/2 cups) olive oil
1 onion, finely chopped
2 garlic cloves, grated
25 g (1 oz) stale bread
30 g (1 oz/scant ¼ cup) blanched almonds
pinch of saffron threads
300 ml (10 fl oz/1¼ cups) fish stock
150 ml (5 fl oz/scant ⅔ cup) full-fat (whole) milk
500 g (1 lb 2 oz) piece salt cod, soaked for 24 hours in several changes of cold water, then chopped into 3-cm (1¼-in) pieces
75 g (2 ½ oz/generous ½ cup) plain flour
a good pinch of pimentón de la Vera
handful of chopped flat-leaf parsley
extra virgin olive oil, for drizzling
sea salt and freshly ground black pepper

Put 4 of the eggs into a pan of cold water and bring to the boil. Boil for 6 minutes, then run under cold water to cool. Peel and cut in half.

Heat 4 tablespoons of the olive oil in a frying pan over a low heat and gently fry the onion and garlic for 10 minutes until lovely and soft. Add the bread and fry for a couple of minutes more until lightly golden.

Transfer this mixture to a large pestle and mortar (or you can use a food processor) and crush with the almonds and plenty of salt and pepper to form a thick *picada*.

Place a wide sauté pan over a medium heat and add the *picada* and saffron. Cook for a few minutes, then gradually add the fish stock, stirring until it forms a thick sauce. Blitz with a hand-held blender until smooth (or transfer to a blender and then return to the pan). Stir in the milk and simmer for 10 minutes until you have a silky golden sauce.

Beat the remaining egg in a dish. Put the flour in a second dish and season with salt, pepper and the pimentón.

Pour the remaining oil into a deep saucepan over a medium heat. Heat the oil to 180°C (350°F), or until a cube of bread turns golden in around 30 seconds. Dust the cod and egg halves in the seasoned flour, then coat all over in the beaten egg before coating again in the flour. Working in batches, deep-fry for 3–4 minutes until golden and crisp. Set aside on a plate lined with paper towels while you fry the rest.

Put the deep-fried fish and egg pieces into the sauce and cook for 1 minute, then scatter over the parsley. Drizzle with extra virgin olive oil and serve.

HAKE WITH SLOW-COOKED ONIONS AND TOMATO SALSA

My mother used to cook this recipe almost every week, mainly because it was a favourite dish of my dad's. Antonio, my dad, had the most amazing smile, and I always remember how it could light up the room, especially when he had his family around him – and even more so when Mum served this up. Slow-cooking the onions releases the sugars and caramelises them, making them a beautiful complement to the tomato salsa. Hake is one of my favourite kinds of fish, and lends itself so well to this balanced, sophisticated sauce. Although leftovers of this dish were rare, my mum would use any we did have to make the most amazing croquettes (see page 79).

INGREDIENTS

100 ml (3½ fl oz/scant
   ½ cup) olive oil
3 large onions, finely sliced
1 bay leaf
150 ml (5 fl oz/scant ⅔ cup)
   white wine
150 ml (5 fl oz/scant ⅔ cup)
   vegetable stock
4 hake fillets (200–250 g/
   7–9 oz each)
sea salt and freshly ground
   black pepper
handful of fresh basil leaves,
   to serve

TOMATO SALSA

500 g (1 lb 2 oz) fresh ripe
   tomatoes, finely chopped
½ small red onion, finely
   chopped
2 tablespoons capers (baby
   capers), chopped
3 tablespoons extra virgin
   olive oil

Heat the oil in a deep lidded sauté pan over a medium heat. Add the onions and bay leaf and season well. Cook for 10 minutes, then cover and cook for a further 30 minutes until really softened but not very coloured.

Meanwhile, make the salsa. Mix all the ingredients together in a bowl, then season well and set aside.

Add the wine to the onions and bubble for 1 minute, then add the stock. Simmer, uncovered, for 10–12 minutes, then season the hake fillets and nestle them into the onions. Reduce the heat to medium-low, cover and gently steam cook for 10 minutes. Turn off the heat and rest for 2–3 minutes.

Drizzle the salsa all over the fish and juicy onions, then scatter with basil leaves before serving.

DEEP-FRIED CALAMARI SANDWICH

For me, this is best sandwich in the world, and (top tip) it's the most incredible hangover food! People seem surprised to learn that some of the best and freshest seafood in Spain can be found in Madrid. I have such wonderful memories of working there in my early twenties. I had a brilliant time exploring the night life and partying, and then discovering places to get something to eat afterwards – this was the best way to discover some incredible street food. One of my favourite places in Madrid is El Mercado de San Miguel, partly because I had one of the best *bocadillo de calamares* of my life there. I think this recipe comes close to it – but I warn you, there's no turning back!

AIOLI

1 free-range egg yolk
1 garlic clove, crushed
finely grated zest of 1 lemon, plus juice to taste
1 teaspoon white wine vinegar or apple cider vinegar
pinch of sea salt
150 ml (5 fl oz/scant ⅔ cup) olive oil

CALAMARI

1 litre (34 fl oz/4 cups) vegetable oil or light olive oil, for deep-frying
120 g (4 oz/scant 1 cup) plain (all-purpose) flour
1 teaspoon pimentón de la Vera
500 g (1 lb 2 oz) small squid, cleaned, tentacles removed and body sliced into rings
1 crusty baguette, cut into 4 pieces and each one halved
sea salt and freshly ground black pepper

Begin by making the aioli. In a bowl, whisk together the egg yolk, garlic, lemon zest and vinegar. Season with a good pinch of sea salt. Slowly drizzle in the olive oil, whisking constantly, until you have a thick, luscious aioli. Add lemon juice to taste and set aside.

To prepare the calamari, pour the oil into a large saucepan (you want it to be half full). Heat to 190°C (375°F), or until a cube of bread browns in 20 seconds. While the oil is heating, mix together the flour and pimentón in a large bowl and season with plenty of sea salt and freshly ground black pepper. Add the squid and toss until well coated in the seasoned flour.

Working in batches, fry the squid for around 3 minutes or until golden and crunchy, then remove from the oil and set aside to drain on a plate lined with paper towels. Sprinkle with salt as soon as you remove it from the oil, then continue with the next batch. Lightly toast the baguette slices, then assemble the sandwiches by spreading the aioli over four of the slices, then adding the fried calamari. Top each one with the remaining baguette slices and enjoy.

MUSSELS WITH TOMATO, PEPPER AND HERB RELISH

As I write this, I am transported to my patio garden at home, picturing myself enjoying a cold glass of sherry with a whole plate of these stunning mussels in front of me. This *tapa* is very popular all over Spain. Normally, the peppers would be roughly chopped and raw, but I prefer to grill (broil) them. For me, this softens the flavour, making the dish much more delicate and offering a greater balance of acidity and sweetness. I think this way of doing it shows proper respect to the unique and awesome flavour of mussels.

INGREDIENTS

500 g (1 lb 2 oz) fresh mussels, cleaned
100 ml (3½ fl oz/scant ½ cup) fino sherry, plus extra to serve
1 red (bell) pepper
200 g (7 oz) ripe tomatoes, finely chopped
1 small shallot, finely chopped
pinch of dried chilli (hot pepper) flakes
1 tablespoon Moscatel vinegar
1 tablespoon extra virgin olive oil
1 teaspoon finely chopped flat-leaf parsley
sea salt and freshly ground black pepper

Put a large, lidded pan over a high heat. Tip in the mussels and add the sherry to create steam, then cover and cook for 4–5 minutes until they are all opened. Tip the mussels into a colander over a bowl to catch the juice. Discard any that haven't opened, then leave to cool.

Blacken the pepper over a flame using tongs, or under a high grill (broiler). Pop it into a plastic zip-lock bag and seal. Leave to steam for 10 minutes, then remove from the bag and peel off the skin.

Deseed the pepper and finely chop the flesh. Tip into a bowl, then add the tomatoes, along with the remaining ingredients. Season well.

Once the mussels are at room temperature, remove the meat from the shells. Remove half of each shell and discard, then arrange the other halves on a serving plate and place a mussel into each one.

Strain 1–2 tablespoons of the mussel juices into the salsa and stir, then spoon this mixture over the mussels. Serve with chilled fino sherry.

THE SPANISH HOME KITCHEN

SEARED SAFFRON MONKFISH WITH BLACK-EYED BEANS

Black-eyed beans are known as carillas in Spanish, but in some areas of the country they call them 'niños con chaleco', which literally means 'kids with vests'. I suppose they might look a bit like that, but I can't really see it personally, nor do I have any idea where the name came from: that's just what they call them. Anyway, this recipe is very close to my heart because it was one of my dad's favourite dishes. He would always smile when this came to the table. My mum wouldn't have made it with monkfish at home: she just used to serve the beans as starter. Obviously, doing it that way makes it vegetarian, but if you want something extra – and I highly recommend it – fry some chorizo just before the onions: it will take the dish to the next level!

INGREDIENTS

150 g (5 oz) black-eyed beans, soaked overnight in cold water
6 tablespoons olive oil
1 onion, finely chopped
2 garlic cloves, grated
50 g (2 oz) coriander (cilantro), stalks and leaves separated and chopped
1 teaspoons ground cumin
1 teaspoon sweet smoked pimentón de la Vera
good pinch of cayenne pepper
400 g (14 oz) large vine tomatoes, chopped
100 ml (3½ fl oz/scant ½ cup) vegetable stock
good pinch of saffron threads
4 x 200 g (7 oz) monkfish fillets
extra virgin olive oil, for drizzling
sea salt and freshly ground black pepper

Put the beans in a large saucepan and cover with cold salted water. Bring to the boil, then reduce to a simmer and cook for 40–50 minutes until they are just tender. Drain well.

Return the now-empty saucepan to the hob and heat 3 tablespoons of the oil over a low heat. Add the onion and gently fry for 10 minutes until softened. Add the garlic, chopped coriander (cilantro) stalks and ground spices and fry for a few minutes more. Add the tomatoes and cook for another 5 minutes, then pour in the stock and season well. Return the drained beans to the pan and cook for 10–12 minutes.

Meanwhile, in a small saucepan, gently heat 2 tablespoons of the oil with the saffron over a low heat, then set aside to infuse.

Heat the remaining 1 tablespoon of oil in a frying pan over a high heat. Add the monkfish and fry for 4–5 minutes on each side until golden and just cooked.

Stir the chopped coriander leaves through the beans and spoon into bowls. Drizzle with extra virgin olive oil, then place a monkfish fillet in each bowl and drizzle over the saffron oil. Finish with a good grinding of black pepper and serve.

TUNA TORTILLA

This is a classic, and a dish we cook regularly at home in London, just as we would in Talaván. I've had it on the menu at José Tapas Bar, too, and it's always extremely popular. I love to eat this either hot or cold, with a strong extra virgin olive oil mayonnaise. My mother's version of this dish is simpler, with just egg and tuna, resulting in the flatter style of tortilla preferred in northern Spain. A top tip is to always use good-quality, fresh eggs: my mum's are normally from her hens, laid just that morning, so she's got an unfair advantage! Whether you make it her way or my way, it's just delicious.

INGREDIENTS

120 ml (4 fl oz/½ cup) extra
   virgin olive oil
1 onion, very finely sliced
2 garlic cloves, finely chopped
220 g (8 oz) jar tuna steaks in
   olive oil, drained
1 tablespoon finely chopped
   flat-leaf parsley
5 free-range eggs
sea salt and freshly ground
   black pepper

Pour 3 tablespoons of the olive oil into a large frying pan (skillet) over a medium-low heat. Add the onion and cook for 10–15 minutes until really lovely and soft. Add the garlic and cook for a few minutes more.

Tip into a bowl and add the tuna. Flake up the tuna with a fork and mix everything together. Stir in the parsley.

In a separate bowl, beat the eggs, then pour them over the onion-and-tuna mixture and season well.

Pour the remaining oil into an 18–20 cm (7–8 in) non-stick frying pan (skillet) over a high heat. When the oil is hot, add the egg mixture. Swirl the pan until the mixture starts to set around the edges, then reduce the heat to medium-low and cook for 4–5 minutes until the tortilla just starts to set. The bottom and sides should be golden, but the middle will still be quite loose.

Cover the pan with a flat lid or board and carefully turn out the tortilla on to it. Don't worry that it is still quite runny, it will all come back together when you continue to cook it. Slide the tortilla back into the pan and, over a low heat, use a spatula to tuck the edges under to give it its characteristic curved look. Cook for a couple more minutes, then turn out on to a board and serve. It should still be lovely and juicy in the middle when you cut into it.

THE SPANISH HOME KITCHEN

RICE AND CLAMS

I'm often asked to share the secret of how I make my rice dishes so intense and full of flavour. The answer is, there's not really any secret! It's very simple: you just need a good *sofrito*, amazing stock, a perfect rice and then anything else you want to add! This recipe is a great example of how, with just a few ingredients, you can make a very happy meal in a short time. We often cook this at home when we fancy something that tastes a bit special, but don't want to spend too long over it. It's a dish you can make throughout the year: we find it goes down just as well at mid-summer garden lunches as it does at autumn or winter dinner parties. People love the simplicity of it, and it's like a warm hug. In a way, it's comfort food, but mouth-wateringly good – and healthy, too.

INGREDIENTS

2 tablespoons olive oil
1 banana shallot, finely chopped
2 garlic cloves, finely sliced
1 fresh bay leaf
2 teaspoons tomato
    purée (paste)
300 g (10½ oz/1⅓ cups) Bomba
    rice or other short-grain rice
750 ml (25 fl oz/3 cups) fresh
    fish broth or stock
handful of fresh marjoram
    leaves
500 g (1 lb 2 oz) clams, cleaned
sea salt and freshly ground
    black pepper

Heat the oil in a shallow casserole dish (Dutch oven) or paella pan over a low heat. Add the shallot and fry for 5 minutes to soften. Add the garlic, bay leaf and tomato purée (paste) and fry for 1 minute more.

Stir in the rice, then increase the heat to medium-high. Toast the rice in the oil for 1 minute, then add the broth, marjoram leaves and plenty of seasoning. Stir and cover, then reduce the heat to low and simmer for 12 minutes until the rice is almost cooked and still lovely and soupy.

Add the clams, then cover once more and cook for a further 4 minutes until the clams are open (discard any that remain closed). Serve.

SLOW-COOKED SQUID

WITH CARAMELISED FENNEL, ONIONS AND A LEMONY PARSLEY DRESSING

There's just something about squid that always gets the party started. Almost every year, our whole family comes together for a week or two in the summer, and mostly you'll find us eating, or talking about food and wine. My partner Peter, who's from the UK, often jokes that my family wakes up thinking about food. We plan lunch at breakfast, then at lunch (which can be a long meal), we're talking about what we're going to have for dinner . . . and so on. It's true, though – we're totally obsessed! In my family, the rules for cooking squid are pretty straightforward. It's cooked in one of only two ways – very quick or very slow! Here, I suggest cooking it very s l o w l y, *despacito*. Slower cooking will help the flavours merge together nicely, especially the incredible sweetness from the onions and the fennel. *¡Madre Mia!* It's fantastic. For me, it's best served in a soup plate or bowl. Just put a slice of sourdough bread in the bottom, then add the squid, with the sauce and the dressing on top – heaven on a plate!

INGREDIENTS

75 ml (2½ fl oz/5 tablespoons)
  olive oil
2 large onions, finely sliced
1 fennel bulb, very finely sliced,
  fronds reserved (see below)
800 ml (27 fl oz/3½ cups)
  vegetable stock
4 lemon thyme sprigs
4 small squid, cleaned
  and sliced
sea salt and freshly ground
  black pepper

LEMON AND PARSLEY DRESSING

handful of flat-leaf parsley, very
  finely chopped
reserved fennel fronds,
  finely chopped
finely grated zest of 1 lemon,
  plus a squeeze of juice
4–5 tablespoons extra virgin
  olive oil

Heat the olive oil in a deep pan over a medium heat. Add the onions and fennel and season well. Fry for 10 minutes, then add the stock, thyme and squid. Bring to the boil, then cover and reduce the heat to low. Simmer for 40 minutes until the onions and squid are really tender.

Take off the lid and remove the squid. Set aside on a plate, then continue to cook the onions and fennel over a medium-high heat for 10–12 minutes until they are a deep golden colour and lovely and sticky.

Meanwhile, make the dressing by putting the ingredients in a food processor and blending together. Season and set aside.

Once the onions are lovely and sticky, you can return the squid to the pan for 3-4 minutes to warm through.

Divide the onion-and-squid mixture between plates, then drizzle with the dressing and serve.

BARBECUED MACKEREL WITH A BLOOD ORANGE AND WATERCRESS SALAD

People often say that things cooked on a barbecue taste better, and I tend to agree – especially when it comes to barbecued mackerel. All those aromatic oils burning against the hot iron, and that beautiful, crispy skin – it's truly divine. The orange and watercress salad here is a perfect match for the deep flavours of the mackerel. You can just use really good, normal, juicy oranges, as long as they're sweet, but, when they're in season, blood oranges are the ideal. Interestingly, they were never very popular in Spain when I was growing up, but that's probably because juicy, fat, sweet oranges were so plentiful. My dad used to be horrified when he came to London and saw not only the price of citrus fruit, but also how different the flavour was. Anyway, the moral of the story is: try to use blood oranges. They're sweeter, and have a subtle depth that works perfectly with more intense, meaty fishes.

INGREDIENTS

4 large fresh mackerel, cleaned
pared zest of 2 blood oranges
4 fresh bay leaves
8 oregano sprigs
olive oil, for drizzling

BLOOD ORANGE AND WATERCRESS SALAD

½ red cabbage, very finely
  shredded
2 blood oranges
1 lemon
½ teaspoon cumin seeds
3 tablespoons extra virgin
  olive oil
200 g (7 oz) watercress leaves

Light your barbecue with a small amount of coals: you want it to burn hot, but not for very long.

Meanwhile, make the salad. Put the cabbage in a bowl. Segment the oranges and the lemon and add to the bowl, along with the cumin seeds and extra virgin olive oil. Toss well and leave to macerate for 15 minutes or so.

Take the mackerel and stuff each one with some orange zest, a bay leaf and two oregano sprigs. Brush all over with oil and put them into a barbecue fish rack if you have one.

When the barbecue is ready, cook the mackerel over the hot coals for 4–5 minutes on each side until just cooked and lightly charred.

Add the watercress leaves to the salad and toss well to combine, then serve with the mackerel.

NOTE

You'll need to leave at least 15 minutes to marinate the salad, so that the cabbage can take on the flavours.

PAN-FRIED COD WITH CHORIZO, WILD MUSHROOMS AND A POACHED EGG

The cod I use in my restaurants is from Norway. There's something magical about the cold, clean Norwegian waters, which are home to the most incredible fish. I have been lucky enough to visit Norway and go fishing for skrei, the migrating cod that come from the Barents Sea to spawn along the coast of Norway. This was one of the most incredible experiences of my life, and I feel so honoured to have done it. Cod is easily one of the most beautiful kinds of fish, but it's important not overcook it (which so many people do), as you risk killing the subtle layers of sea flavours. Funnily enough, fresh cod is really hard to find in Spanish markets – in fact, I can't remember ever seeing it there! What is very popular – and, I have to say, always in my mum's fridge at home – is salted cod. So, if you can't get fresh cod, salted cod is absolutely fine to use here.

INGREDIENTS

6 tablespoons olive oil
300 g (10½ oz) wild mushrooms such as *níscalo* (saffron milk cap) mushrooms or girolles
1 garlic clove, finely sliced
200 g (7 oz) stale bread, diced
200 g (7 oz) chorizo, diced
150 g (5 oz) tomatoes, chopped
4 cod fillets (about 200 g/7 oz each)
4 free-range eggs
handful of flat-leaf parsley, finely chopped
sea salt and freshly ground black pepper

Heat 2 tablespoons of the oil in a frying pan (skillet) over a high heat and fry the mushrooms and garlic for 6–8 minutes until golden and crisp. Season, then scoop out of the pan and set aside on a plate.

Add a further 2 tablespoons of the oil to the pan and fry the bread for 2–3 minutes until golden, then transfer to the plate with the mushrooms. Now add the chorizo to the pan and fry for 5 minutes until the fat has been released and the chorizo is golden. Add the tomatoes and plenty of seasoning and cook for another few minutes, then turn off the heat.

Meanwhile, season the cod and heat the remaining oil in a separate frying pan. Fry, skin-side down, for 3–4 minutes until golden. At the same time, poach the eggs in a pan of barely simmering water.

Flip the fish over and fry for 2 minutes on the other side until just cooked and golden.

Return the mushrooms and fried bread to the first frying pan and toss with the tomatoey chorizo. Divide this mixture between 4 plates, then top each one with a golden cod fillet and a poached egg. Scatter with parsley and serve.

TWO WAYS WITH PRAWNS

I think everyone loves prawns, and everyone has their favourite type. These two recipes are my preferred ways to make them, and I just love them like this. I was cooking at home in Talaván some years ago, having a great time with my family. The kids (I still call them 'the kids', but the youngest is twenty years old now), couldn't decide how they wanted the prawns – I'd offered them grilled or *al ajillo*. I always like to see them happy, so in the end I made them both ways. Both the recipes and methods here are really simple, but they're also amazing in their own unique ways – a bit like the kids, my nephews and nieces! I don't have a favourite use here.

GRILLED KING PRAWNS

SERVES 4 AS A TAPA

TAKES 15 MINUTES

INGREDIENTS

12 large tiger prawns, left whole/unpeeled
2 tablespoons olive oil
juice of ½ lemon
sea salt and freshly ground black pepper

Prepare a barbecue with good-quality charcoal and light it. Wait until it is really hot. Alternatively, you can heat a griddle pan over a high heat.

Drizzle the oil over the prawns and season generously, then cook on the barbecue or in the griddle pan for 4–6 minutes, turning once, until the prawns turn pink all over.

Transfer to a plate and squeeze over the lemon juice. Serve immediately – and don't forget to suck the heads to get all their delicious juices.

PRAWNS WITH GARLIC AND FLAT-LEAF PARSLEY

SERVES 4 AS A TAPA

TAKES 15 MINUTES

INGREDIENTS

300 g (10½ oz) large prawns
100 ml (3½ fl oz/scant ½ cup) olive oil
2 garlic cloves, finely chopped
pinch of hot smoked pimentón de la Vera
handful of flat-leaf parsley, leaves picked and chopped
bread, to serve

Peel the prawns, then run the tip of a sharp knife along the back of each one and remove the vein. Pat them dry with paper towels.

Heat the oil in a heavy-based frying pan over a high heat.

Add the prawns to the pan and cook for 2–3 minutes, or until pink all over, turning once. Add the garlic and pimentón and cook for a few seconds more, then tip into a warm bowl. Scatter the parsley over the top and toss to coat. Serve with crusty bread.

THE SPANISH HOME KITCHEN

CRAB CANELONES

One of our favourite pasta dishes to have at home is crab linguine: Peter and I get cravings for this sometimes, and we just have to have it. It's so easy to prepare, and always delicious. When I make these canelones, with lots of garlic, chilli, white and brown crab meat and parsley, it makes me think of crab linguine; and when I make crab linguine, I think of these. It's not just the flavours and ingredients they share; both dishes make me very happy too. Canelones are a cylindrical type of pasta. They are classically Spanish and very popular in Cataluña, but surprisingly, they're also popular in my home town, Talaván! I think one day I will be very greedy and cook both linguine and canelones to enjoy at the same time. Why not?

BECHAMEL SAUCE

45 ml (1½ fl oz/3 tablespoons) olive oil
45g (1¾ oz/generous ⅓ cup) plain (all-purpose) flour
500 ml (17 fl oz/2 cups) fresh shellfish or chicken stock
300 ml (10 fl oz/1¼ cups) double (heavy) cream
good grating of fresh nutmeg
80 g (3 oz) finely grated Manchego, plus extra to top

FILLING

60 ml (2 fl oz/¼ cup) olive oil
1 small shallot, finely chopped
2 red chillies, finely chopped
3 garlic cloves, finely sliced
50 g (2 oz) brown crab meat
500 g (1 lb 2 oz) ripe tomatoes, diced
150 ml (5 fl oz/scant ⅔ cup) fresh shellfish or chicken stock
500 g (1 lb 2 oz) white crab meat
15 g (½ oz) tarragon, finely chopped
250 g (9 oz) dried canelloni pasta tubes
sea salt and freshly ground black pepper

Preheat the oven to 190°C/170°C fan/375°F/gas 5.

To make the bechamel, heat the oil in a saucepan over a medium heat. Add the flour and cook for a minute or two, then gradually stir in the stock until you have a smooth, thick sauce. Add the cream, nutmeg and cheese and season to taste. Set aside.

In a separate pan, heat the oil over a very low heat. Very gently cook the shallot, chillies and garlic for a good 15 minutes.

Increase the heat to medium high and add the brown crab meat and fry for 1 minute, then add the tomatoes and stock. Season and cook for 12–15 minutes, then take off the heat. Stir in the white crab meat and tarragon.

Blanch the pasta tubes in a pan of boiling water for 3 minutes, then drain and cool under running water.

Put a spoonful of the crab filling into each of the pasta tubes. Fit the filled tubes snugly into an ovenproof dish, then pour over the bechamel. Scatter over a little more cheese, then bake for 25–30 minutes until golden and bubbling. Serve with a green salad.

CLAMS IN SPICY TOMATO SAUCE

For me, clams are such a beautiful thing to cook – and, of course, to eat. I really love these sweet little shellfish, as they're so succulent and versatile. With so many different types of clams available, it's exciting to explore different ways to cook with them – or you can even just eat them raw. When I was a child, when we would travel down to Andalusia, our neighbouring region, to visit extended family, my mum would cook clams simply with Fino sherry, and we'd enjoy them with a rice dish.

Here, I'm using different spices, which at first you might think are too strong and will take away from the flavour of the clams. Don't worry, this is not the case. Follow the recipe and cook the clams properly bring out those flavours of the sea, and then you'll notice how well this goes with the heat from the chillies. Just perfect.

INGREDIENTS

3 dried ancho chillies
small pinch of dried chilli (hot pepper) flakes
1 teaspoon cumin seeds, lightly toasted
½ teaspoon sweet smoked pimentón de la Vera
2 garlic cloves, peeled
1 tablespoon red wine vinegar
3 tablespoons olive oil
800 g (1 lb 12 oz) tomatoes, chopped
75 ml (3½ fl oz/scant ½ cup) water
2 kg (4 lb 8 oz) clams, cleaned
small handful of flat-leaf parsley, chopped
crusty bread, to serve

Rehydrate the ancho chillies in hot water for 20 minutes, then deseed them and put in a heavy pestle and mortar or small food processor. Add the chilli flakes, toasted cumin seeds, pimentón, garlic and vinegar. Season and mash or whizz to a paste, adding a splash of water to loosen.

Heat the olive oil in a saucepan over a medium heat. Add the chilli paste and cook for 5 minutes, then add the tomatoes and 75 ml (2½ fl oz/⅓ cup) water. Cook for 10 minutes.

When the sauce is almost ready, heat a large, lidded heavy-based pan over a high heat. Add the clams and 100 ml (3½ fl oz/scant ½ cup) water and cover to steam for 1–2 minutes until the shells open. Remove and discard any that do not open and then tip the clams, along with their juices, into the spicy tomato sauce. Toss well and scatter with parsley. Serve with crusty bread.

OCTOPUS SALAD

Pimentón de la Vera is the most popular spice at my mother Isabel's house. In fact, I think it's the most popular spice in almost every house in Spain. It must be the smokiness and intensity of the flavour that makes you fall in love with it. I also love the gorgeous little tins it comes in. There are so many different ones in circulation, and all of them are really pretty. I like nothing more than coming into a kitchen in Spain and seeing those little containers decorating the shelves! I personally have three different designs: the first two are in the honour of the patroness of my village in Talaván, La Virgen del Río, and the most recent one follows my latest brand design. They are stunning, all of them, but the best thing of all is what's inside: pimentón de la Vera. I'm very proud that my own pimentón has been awarded two stars by the Great Taste Awards, a true sign of quality.

INGREDIENTS

1 kg (2 lb 4 oz) sustainably
  sourced octopus
1 lemon, halved
100 ml (3½ fl oz/scant ½ cup)
  white wine
500 g (1 lb 2 oz) new potatoes,
  halved or quartered
150 g (5 oz) green beans
olive oil, for drizzling
1 celery heart, finely sliced
handful of celery leaves,
  roughly chopped
sea salt and freshly ground
  black pepper

DRESSING

90 ml (3 fl oz/⅓ cup) extra
  virgin olive oil
2 garlic cloves, sliced
good pinch of chilli flakes
1 teaspoon sweet smoked
  pimentón de la Vera
finely pared zest of 1 lemon
4 tablespoons red wine vinegar

Put the octopus in a large wide and deep saucepan or casserole (Dutch oven) with the lemon halves and wine. Pour over enough water to just cover. Bring to the boil, then reduce the heat to low. Cover and simmer for about an hour (or until very tender). Drain.

Meanwhile, put the potatoes in a saucepan of cold salted water and bring to the boil. Simmer for 20–25 minutes until very tender but not falling apart, then drain in a colander and cover with a tea towel to steam.

In a separate pan, cook the beans in slightly salted water for 10 minutes until they are lovely and soft. Drain well.

Once the octopus is cooked, separate the tentacles and drizzle with oil, then season. Heat a frying pan or griddle pan over a high heat and sear the tentacles for 2–3 minutes until lightly charred.

In a large serving bowl, toss the octopus with the lovely tender potatoes, beans and celery.

For the dressing, heat the oil in a small saucepan over a low heat and add the garlic, chilli, pimentón and lemon zest. Once hot, add the vinegar season well. Pour the dressing over the salad, scatter over the celery leaves and serve.

TUNA, MONKFISH AND MUSSEL STEW WITH ROMESCO TOASTS

I am a huge fan of romesco, and yes, I confess I do use it a lot in my cooking. Obviously, it's the essential accompaniment to calçots when they are in season, and it's great with grilled fish, meat and vegetables. It's also delicious as a dressing for salads, or served simply on toast, as I'm doing here.

ROMESCO TOASTS

300 g (10½ oz) ripe vine
  tomatoes, quartered
3 tablespoons olive oil,
  for drizzling and frying
30 g (1 oz/scant ¼ cup)
  blanched almonds
20 g (¾ oz) stale sourdough
  bread, torn
1 garlic clove, peeled
2 teaspoons nora pepper paste
2 teaspoons PX sherry vinegar
3 tablespoons extra virgin
  olive oil
1 crusty baguette, sliced

TUNA, MONKFISH AND MUSSEL STEW

3 tablespoons olive oil, plus
  extra for brushing
1 large onion, finely chopped
2 garlic cloves, finely sliced
1 fennel bulb, finely sliced
good pinch of saffron
1 teaspoon hot smoked
  pimentón de la Vera
700 g (1 lb 9 oz) tomatoes,
  chopped
500 g (1 lb 2 oz) small new
  potatoes
800 ml (27 fl oz/3½ cups) water
400 g (14 oz) tuna steak
600 g (1 lb 5 oz) monkfish, cut
  into chunks
1 kg (2 lb 4 oz) mussels, cleaned
small handful of flat-leaf
  parsley, chopped
sea salt and freshly ground
  black pepper

For the romesco sauce, preheat the oven to 220°C/200°C fan/425°F/gas 7. Place the tomatoes in a baking dish and drizzle with a little of the olive oil. Season well, then toss and roast for 30 minutes.

Heat the rest of the olive oil in a frying pan over a medium heat. Add the nuts and fry for 2–3 minutes until golden. Scoop out with a slotted spoon and set aside. Add the torn sourdough to the pan and fry for 3–4 minutes until golden, then add the garlic, tomatoes, nora paste and vinegar. Fry for 1–2 minutes, then transfer to a food processor with the nuts and pulse until smooth but still chunky. Drizzle with the oil.

For the stew, heat the oil in a deep saucepan over a low heat. Add the onion, garlic and fennel and gently fry for 10 minutes. Add the saffron, pimentón and tomatoes and cook for another minute or two. Take your potatoes and insert the tip of a sharp knife into the centre of each one. Twist the knife so that the potato cracks open giving a jagged edge, which helps release the starch into the stew. Add the potatoes and water to the stew.

Season well and bring to the boil, then reduce to a simmer and cook for 20 minutes.

Heat a heavy-based frying pan over a high heat. Brush the tuna steak with oil and season well. Add to the frying pan and sear briefly on each side.

Cut the seared tuna into pieces and add to the stew, along with the monkfish. Cook for 3–4 minutes, then add the mussels. Cover and cook for 1–2 minutes until they open, discard any that are closed.

Spread the romesco over the baguette slices. Spoon the stew into bowls and top with the toasts. Serve scattered with parsley.

CRISPY FRIED SEA BREAM AND BONES

WITH TOMATO SALAD AND ROAST GARLIC AIOLI

In Andalusia you will find fried fish everywhere, served on big platters with lots of different fish, from gorgeous red mullet and cuttlefish to boquerones and squid. When served with a cold beer or glass of Manzanilla sherry, it's a match made in heaven! But in in El Faro del Puerto, a restaurant in El Puerto de Santa María, my friend Fernado makes this recipe with a fish called 'borriquete', which roughly translates as little donkey! It is a very local fish that I've never seen here in the markets; it's an oily fish with firm meat. As we don't see borriquete in our waters, bream make a very good substitute.

AIOLI

125 ml (4¼ fl oz/½ cup) olive oil, plus extra for drizzling
1 garlic bulb
2 teaspoons white wine vinegar
1 free-range egg yolk
25 ml (¾ fl oz) extra virgin olive oil
lemon juice, to taste

SALAD

500 g (1 lb 2 oz) tomatoes, sliced
½ red onion, finely sliced
1 tablespoon capers
2 teaspoons sherry vinegar
3 tablespoons extra virgin olive oil
1 tablespoon oregano

SEA BREAM

1 x 700 g (1 lb 9 oz) sea bream, cleaned
75 g (2 ½ oz/⅔ cup) chickpea (gram) flour
1 teaspoon sweet pimentón de la Vera
1 teaspoon hot smoked pimentón de la Vera
1 teaspoon ground cumin
500 ml (17 fl oz/2 cups) olive oil or vegetable oil, for deep-frying
sea salt and freshly ground black pepper

Preheat the oven to 180°C/160°C fan/375°F/gas 4.

Begin by making the aioli. Drizzle some olive oil over the garlic bulb and rub it in, then roast for 40 minutes until tender.

Once cool enough to handle, squeeze the roasted garlic cloves out of their skins into a bowl and whisk with the white wine vinegar and egg yolk. Season well, then whisk in the olive oil until you have a thick, glossy mayonnaise. Whisk in the extra virgin olive oil and a splash of just-boiled water. Add lemon juice to taste and set aside.

To make the salad, mix the tomatoes with the red onion and capers in a bowl. Drizzle with the vinegar and oil, and season well with salt, pepper and oregano.

Remove the fillets from the fish and dice the meat into small cubes. Clean the cavity of the fish.

Pour the oil for deep-frying into a wide sauté pan over a medium-high heat and heat to 180°C/350°F, or until a cube of bread turns golden brown in around 30 seconds.

In a shallow dish, mix the chickpea (gram) flour with the spices and season with salt and pepper. Dust the cubed fish and the fish bones in the flour. Fry the bones for 5 minutes until golden and crisp, then set aside to drain on plate lined with paper towels. Fry the cubed fish for 3–4 minutes until golden and tender.

Serve the crispy fish and bones with the tomato salad and the aioli.

POTATOES WITH RICE AND SALTED COD

At end of summer, when the seasons are changing, my mum makes her impressive chilli pepper ristra (a bundle of vegetables hung up to dry), which will last for the whole year. I've always loved to see them drying on the terrace: to me, they represent proper rural Spain. We start using the chillies as early as the autumn. The picture of this dish was taken on a gorgeous autumnal afternoon on my brother and sister-in-law's land, and it was a beautiful day. My mum cooked the dish, and it was the first time she'd used her peppers that year: it was spectacular. I've been cooking this dish next to her for many years, and in this recipe I've tried to capture her method exactly. I think it's almost the same, but you know … I'm sure she adds something when I'm not looking to take it to that (M)other dimension. I don't know what it is; I really don't.

INGREDIENTS

800 g (1 lb 12 oz) salt cod loin
3 tablespoons olive oil
2 onions, finely sliced
3 garlic cloves, finely sliced
1 teaspoon smoked bittersweet
    pimentón de la Vera
2 fresh bay leaves
5 mild dried guindilla peppers,
    snipped into 2 or 3 pieces
300 g (10½ oz) floury potatoes,
    thickly sliced
70 g (2¼ oz) Bomba rice or other
    short-grain rice
750 ml (25 fl oz/3 cups)
    fresh fish, chicken or
    vegetable stock
crusty bread, to serve

Soak the salt cod in cold water for 24 hours, changing the water several times. Remove the skin and any bones or fins from the fish. You will be left with about 500 g (1 lb 2 oz).

Heat the oil in a casserole dish (Dutch oven) over a medium heat and add the onions. Fry for 10 minutes until softened, then add the garlic, pimentón, bay leaves and dried peppers and cook for a few minutes more.

Add the potatoes and rice to the pan and stir to coat well, then add the stock and prepared salt cod. Bring to the boil, then reduce the heat to low and simmer, covered, for 20–25 minutes until the potatoes and rice are tender and the fish is flaking apart. Serve with crusty bread.

RUSSIAN SALAD WITH HOMEMADE CONFIT TUNA

I've tried and tasted many different versions of Russian salad in my life. There are many really great variations, and you can find this salad everywhere from service stations (which can be amazing in Spain, by the way), great tapas bars and restaurants. I have to say that one of the best Russian salads I've ever had is the one made by my sister Isabel – she prepares it very simply, with potatoes, good-quality tinned tuna, peas, green olives, roasted peppers, boiled eggs and plenty of good mayonnaise. In my version here, I'm not using as much mayo as you'd normally find in the dish, keeping it nice and light. I think this way you can really see and taste the individual ingredients. Tinned tuna is great, but if you confit it yourself it is really special.

CONFIT TUNA

500 ml (17 fl oz/2 cups) olive oil
finely pared zest of 1 lemon
10 black peppercorns
1 garlic clove, bashed
350 g (12 oz) fresh alba-
core or yellowfin tuna

SALAD

400 g (14 oz) red-skinned
    potatoes, peeled and cut
    into 1 cm (½ in) cubes
175 g (6 oz) carrots, peeled and
    cut into 1 cm (½ in) cubes
150 g (5 oz) frozen peas
2 free-range eggs
50 g (2 oz) cornichons, chopped
50 g (2 oz) green olives, pitted
    and sliced
    2 tablespoons capers
    150 g (5 oz) piquillo or roasted
    red peppers, sliced
    extra virgin olive oil, for
    drizzling

MAYO

2 free-range egg yolks
1 teaspoon Dijon mustard
2 teaspoons white wine vinegar
250 ml (8½ fl oz/1 cup) olive oil
    (from the confit tuna)
50 ml (1¾ fl oz) extra virgin
    olive oil
lemon juice, to taste

Begin with the confit tuna. Pour the oil into a saucepan over a medium-high heat and heat to 150°C (300°F), or until a cube of bread browns in around 45 seconds. Add the lemon zest, peppercorns and garlic and infuse for 10 minutes. Now add the tuna and cook for 10 minutes until the tuna is tender and just cooked through. Remove from the oil and set aside – remember to save half of the oil for the mayonnaise later.

Put the cubed potatoes into a large saucepan of cold salted water. Bring to the boil and simmer for 3–4 minutes until tender. Drain well. Next, cook the carrots in a saucepan of boiling water for 2–3 minutes, adding the peas for the last minute, then drain and toss with the potatoes in a large bowl. Meanwhile, put the eggs into a pan of cold water, bring to the boil and cook for 6 minutes. Drain and cool under running cold water, peel, chop then set aside.

To make the mayonnaise put the egg yolks, mustard and white wine vinegar into a bowl and whisk together with plenty of seasoning. Gradually whisk in the oil from the confit and then the extra virgin olive oil until you have a thick glossy mayonnaise. Add lemon juice to taste.

Add half of the mayonnaise to the bowl with the potatoes, carrots and peas. Add the chopped egg and two-thirds of the cornichons, olives and capers. Mix well.

Flake the tuna and very gently fold it into the salad. Top with the peppers and the sliced eggs, then scatter over the rest of the cornichons, olives and capers. Drizzle with oil and serve.

MEAT

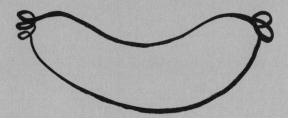

The most important thing about meat is the quality of it. The meat I buy to cook at home and in my restaurants is always meticulously researched, and the provenance fully determined. It's vital to know where our meat comes from, how the animals have been treated and looked after, how and what they've been fed, how much exercise they've had and so on.

Animals are an essential part of our lives, our culture and our economy. To eat meat is fine but it's important to try to get hold of the best quality meat you possibly can. The politics of food changes, and it's no longer okay to eat meat just for the sake of eating meat. Many people avoid meat altogether these days, often related to a sense of wider social responsibility and because there is a lot of poor-quality meat around. I think that to be responsible carnivores, we must know as much as we can about what we're eating. If we are going to continue to enjoy eating meat, we must get hold of truly great meat. Inevitably this is likely to cost a bit more but in terms of taste, it's worth spending a little extra for quality.

When I was a child in my little village, I would look forward so much to Christmas-time for many reasons, one of them being the presents from the three Kings on the 6th January, the day of the kings - Los Reyos Magos. Most of all though, I would love seeing the whole family gather together for the 'Matanza del Cerdo' (loosely translated, slaughter of the pig). My family always did this in the winter, around Christmas-time, and they'd invite friends and family who would come from all over Spain to help with the butchery, making charcuterie, sausages, jamón, and so on. Every time, the proceedings would start as early as a 5.30am, the atmosphere was hushed, it was foggy, and dewy. This was an incredibly special day of the year because everyone would eat and drink together through the day, catching up and having fun. I remember clearly the smell of the smoke drifting from the chimneys, and how exciting it was to see everyone there together. One of the main reasons for having the Matanza was to provide food for our family, extended family, and friends for the entire year ahead. These are precious memories.

PATATERA TOASTS WITH MANCHEGO AND HONEY

Patatera is a type of chorizo that's typical of my area in Extremadura. It's made by combining some of the fat from high-quality pork with various spices and potatoes. I can tell you, the first one of the season is always superb. It's so fresh and soft at that stage that you can spread it thickly on toasted bread, and that is how we'd eat it at home. I'm sharing this recipe exactly as we'd have it, because I want you to know how good it is. It can be a challenge to find good patatera in London, but sobrasada or 'nduja will do the job (almost!) as well. Another brilliant way to eat patatera is to simply wrap it in foil and put it straight on to a hot barbecue. This takes me back to my childhood on our farm in Talaván: just me standing next to the fire, a patatera in the foil, and some bread ready and waiting! It's simple but exquisite.

INGREDIENTS

1 tablespoon olive oil
8 small or 4 large slices of
   slightly stale crusty bread
200 g (7 oz) patatera,
   skin removed 80 g (3 oz)
Manchego shavings
honey, for drizzling

Heat the olive oil in a frying pan over a medium heat. Add the bread and fry for around 2 minutes on each side until golden. Thickly spread the patatera over the toast, then scatter the shaved Manchego over the top and drizzle with a little honey. Serve immediately.

CUCHIFRITO WITH PRESERVED LEMON SALSA

I just adore these crispy, golden pieces of heaven. The word *cuchifrito* comes from 'fried pig', and it's traditionally made with suckling pigs – in my area in Spain, we eat them when they are as young as 21 days old. I sometimes make it with pork belly instead, as that's much easier to source. I'm not sure if my mum would agree with me regarding the lemon salsa, but I know she loves to serve this with a simple tomato salad, dressed with extra virgin olive oil and a really punchy vinegar. My favourite is a good sherry reserve vinegar, but if not, a decent red wine vinegar will do.

INGREDIENTS

2.25 kg (5 lb 8 oz) thin end of
  pork belly (without bones,
  but with cartilage), cut into
  3-cm (1¼-in) chunks
6 fat garlic cloves
large handful of flat-leaf parsley
200 ml (7 fl oz/scant
  1 cup) olive oil
good grinding of black pepper
150 ml (5 fl oz/scant ⅔ cup)
  white wine vinegar
1 litre (34 fl oz/4 cups)
  mild-flavoured olive oil,
  for deep-frying
sea salt and freshly ground
  black pepper

PRESERVED
LEMON SALSA

juice of 1 lemon
3 preserved lemons,
  rinds finely chopped
5 tablespoons capers
  (baby capers), chopped
35 g (1¼ oz) flat-leaf parsley,
  finely chopped
20 g (¾ oz) fresh oregano,
  finely chopped
20 g (¾ oz) mint, finely chopped
1 green chilli, finely diced
150 ml (5 fl oz/scant ⅔ cup)
  extra virgin olive oil

Put the pork belly chunks in a large dish. Mash the garlic with a pestle and mortar and add to the dish, along with the parsley, olive oil, pepper and vinegar. Mix well, then cover and leave to marinate overnight in the fridge.

The next day, preheat the oven to 170°C/150°C fan/340°F/ gas 3½. Transfer the pork belly chunks and their marinade to a roasting tin (pan), then cover with kitchen foil and roast for 1½ hours.

Meanwhile, make the salsa. Simply mix all the ingredients together in a bowl, then season well and set aside.

Once the the pork has finished roasting, pour the oil for deep-frying into a deep pan over a medium-high heat and preheat to 170°C (340°F). If you don't have a thermometer, drop a small cube of bread in the oil – it will brown in about 25–30 seconds when the oil is hot enough. Drain the meat, then, working in batches, fry for 5–6 minutes until the pieces are really golden and crisp. Drain on plate lined with paper towels, then season with salt and pepper. Once all the meat has been fried, serve with the salsa.

TIP

You can order suckling pig online or speak to your local butcher if you want to try this recipe with the real deal.

SPICED BRAISED GOAT WITH AUBERGINES

My favourite thing ever: kid (baby goat) stew, or *caldereta de cabrito*. My mum, Isabel, cooks this for all the most important occasions: it's a truly special dish and would definitely appear at my last supper, served with just some fries and a green salad. Kid meat might not be very easy to find in supermarkets, but you can get it online from various places with next-day delivery. Goat meat really is delicious, and amazing value for money. Normally the meat comes from a female goat, who has been producing milk and then gives us this incredible meat. The whole circle of life.

The aubergine (eggplant) lends a great texture to the dish, and is the perfect flavour pairing with the tender meat.

INGREDIENTS

75 ml (2½ fl oz/5 tablespoons)
   olive oil
1.5 kg (3 lb 5 oz) goat shoulder,
   diced into 5-cm (2-in) chunks
1 large onion, finely sliced
2 teaspoons cumin seeds
1 teaspoon coriander seeds
2 cloves
1 heaped teaspoon fennel seeds
2 teaspoons sweet smoked
   pimentón de la Vera
1 garlic bulb, halved horizontally
1 tablespoon tomato
   purée (paste)
450 ml (15 fl oz/1 cups) red wine
500 ml (17 fl oz/2 cups) good
   fresh chicken stock
2 aubergines (eggplants),
   cut into 3-cm (1½-in) cubes
sea salt and freshly ground
   black pepper
boiled potatoes or crusty bread,
   to serve

Heat 2 tablespoons of the oil in a deep casserole dish (Dutch oven) or heavy-based frying pan (skillet) over a medium-high heat. Add the goat meat and season. Sear the meat all over until browned; you might need to do this in batches, depending on the size of your pan. Remove from the pan and set aside.

Add another tablespoon of the oil to the pan and gently fry the onion for 10 minutes until very soft. Add the spices and the halved garlic and cook for another 1–2 minutes.

Return the meat to the pan, along with the tomato purée (paste) and red wine, and bubble for a few minutes, then add the stock. Cover and bring to the boil, then reduce to a simmer and cook gently for 2½–3 hours.

Heat the rest of the oil in a separate large pan and brown the aubergine (eggplant) all over. Season, then add to the braising goat and cook for a further 30 minutes until the meat is melting and tender. Serve with boiled potatoes or crusty bread.

ROAST GUINEA FOWL WITH PEPITORIA SAUCE, FRIED NEW POTATOES AND GREENS

Pepitoria sauce is usually served with chicken, with the meat slowly stewed in the sauce. It's a popular dish all over Spain, and I do love it, but in this recipe I wanted to show that the sauce can be used in different ways. It's very diverse, and works brilliantly with roasted fish, grilled vegetables and chicken. It's fantastic with guinea fowl, too – and with the potatoes and greens, maybe this can become your new favourite Sunday roast! This is best served with a very good glass of red.

INGREDIENTS

500 g (1 lb 2 oz) new potatoes, halved
2 oven-ready guinea fowl (about 1 kg/2 lb 4 oz each)
3–4 tablespoons olive oil
200 g (7 oz) shredded cavolo nero
extra virgin olive oil, for drizzling
sea salt and freshly ground black pepper

PEPITORIA SAUCE

good pinch of saffron strands
4 tablespoons boiling water
2 tablespoons olive oil
3 garlic cloves, finely sliced
25 g (1 oz) blanched almonds
25 g (1 oz) stale sourdough bread, torn into pieces
small handful of flat-leaf parsley
1 onion, finely chopped
2 small carrots, finely chopped
1 celery stalk, finely chopped
200 ml (7 fl oz/scant 1 cup) fino sherry or white wine
400 ml (13 fl oz/generous 1½ cups) fresh chicken stock
2 bay leaves
½ cinnamon stick
yolk from 1 hardboiled egg

Preheat the oven to 200°C/180°C fan/400°F/gas 6.

Put the potatoes in a large saucepan of cold salted water. Bring to the boil and cook for 6–8 minutes until just tender. Drain the potatoes and tip into a roasting tin (pan). Drizzle them with 1–2 tablespoons olive oil and season.

Add the guinea fowl to the roasting tin and drizzle with the remaining olive oil. Season well. Roast for 1 hour–1 hour 10 minutes, depending on the size of the birds, turning the potatoes once or twice. The potatoes should be golden and the birds should be cooked through with crispy skin.

Meanwhile, make the sauce. Soak the saffron in the boiling water for 10 minutes.

Heat 1 tablespoon of the oil in a saucepan over a low heat and gently fry the garlic for 1 minute, then add the almonds and bread and fry for 4–5 minutes until golden. Transfer to a food processor and blitz with the parsley to make a *picada*.

Add the remaining olive oil to the pan, still over a low heat, and gently fry the onion, carrots and celery for 10 minutes. Add the sherry and bubble for a minute or two, then pour in the stock and saffron, along with the soaking water, and simmer for 10–15 minutes.

Mash the egg yolk with the back of a fork and whisk it into the sauce, then stir in the *picada*. Season and simmer for a few minutes to thicken.

Meanwhile, blanch the cavolo nero in a pan of boiling water for a couple of minutes, then drain and toss with the oil.

Serve the guinea fowl and potatoes with the sauce and greens.

BITTER LEAF SALAD WITH SEARED DUCK BREAST AND APPLE

WITH A BEE POLLEN VINAIGRETTE

In the late 1980s in northern Extremadura, a man called Don Cirilo started selling a very popular energy supplement call Ciripolen – you could say it was known as the viagra of its time! He was a well-known beekeeper in the Las Hurdes area. There was no pharmacy in his village, so he started making a special concoction containing milk, honey, pollen, royal jelly and some herbs foraged from the forest. The drink became very popular across the whole of Spain and the rest of the world.

Bee pollen may not be the most common ingredient, but it's always been in my diet in many different forms. I've had it with breakfasts, marinated fish and meat, and now in this vinaigrette, which really brings all the other ingredients together with stunning, earthy flavours.

INGREDIENTS

2 duck breasts, skin on, skin scored
100 ml (3½ fl oz/scant ½ cup) red vermouth
175 g (6 oz) stale white bread, torn
120 g (4 oz) walnuts
60 g (2 oz/¼ cup) caster (superfine) sugar
2 crisp eating (dessert) apples
½ head frisée lettuce, torn
1 head red endive, leaves separated
1 tablespoon chopped chives
sea salt and freshly ground black pepper

BEE POLLEN VINAIGRETTE

2 tablespoons apple vinegar
1 generous teaspoon honey
1 teaspoon bee pollen granules (or fennel pollen)
3–4 tablespoons extra virgin olive oil

Preheat the oven to 200°C/180°C fan/400°F/gas 6.

Season the duck breasts with salt and pepper. Heat a heavy-based, ovenproof frying pan (skillet) over a medium–high heat. Place the duck breasts in the pan, skin-side down, and cook for 5–6 minutes without moving until the skin is golden and crisp, and the fat has rendered out. Drain the fat from the pan and reserve.

Turn the duck breasts over in the pan, then transfer to the oven and cook for 8 minutes. Remove and transfer to a plate to rest, pouring over any juices from the pan.

Return the pan to the stove over a high heat. Add the vermouth and reduce by half.

In a separate pan, heat the leftover duck fat over a medium heat. Add the torn bread and fry until golden and crisp. Season well and set aside to drain on a paper towel.

Meanwhile, place a clean, dry frying pan over a medium heat and toast the walnuts for 2 minutes. Add the sugar and 1 tablespoon of water, then allow to cook and caramelise for 2–3 minutes. Tip on to a greased baking sheet and set aside to cool, then roughly chop.

To make the vinaigrette, mix together all the ingredients in a jug (pitcher) and season well.

Finely slice the apples, then toss the salad leaves, crispy bread, apples and walnuts together in a large bowl. Pour any of the resting juices from the duck into the dressing, along with the reduced vermouth, and whisk to combine. Thinly slice the duck and arrange over the salad. Scatter over the chives, pour over the dressing and serve.

ROAST PARTRIDGE STUFFED WITH WILD MUSHROOMS AND CHICKEN LIVERS

This recipe travelled from Alcántara to France after famously being stolen from the monastery of Alcántara at the beginning of the 19th century by Napoleon. The monks were very proud of their recipe books, so it was a huge loss for their community. The stolen recipe became very popular in France – Escoffier said was the best trophy of the war! The original recipe, which was called *Perdices al modo de Alcántara* (essentially Alcántara-style partridge) features foie gras and truffles, but I've used chicken livers. This recipe is a treasure – keep it safe!

INGREDIENTS

4 oven-ready partridges
1 tablespoon olive oil
50 g (2 oz) unsalted butter
175 g (6 oz) chicken livers
1 banana shallot, finely chopped
2 garlic cloves, grated
1 bay leaf
100 g (3½ oz) wild mushrooms (or chestnut mushrooms), chopped
60 ml (2 fl oz/¼ cup) port, plus an extra splash
25 g (1 oz) hazelnuts and 25 g (1 oz) almonds, coarsely ground in a pestle and mortar
50 g (2 oz) fresh white breadcrumbs
large handful of flat-leaf parsley
3 thyme sprigs, leaves picked
sea salt and freshly ground black pepper

Preheat the oven to 200°C/180°C fan/400°F/gas 6. Season the partridges inside and out.

Heat the oil and half the butter in a heavy-based frying pan (skillet) over a high heat. Add the chicken livers and sear for 2–3 minutes until browned and just cooked. Scoop out of the pan and set aside in a bowl.

Reduce the heat then add the shallot to the pan and fry gently for 5 minutes, then add the garlic, bay leaf and mushrooms. Increase the heat to medium and fry for a further 4–5 minutes, then add the port and bubble until it is reduced to about 2 tablespoons of liquid. Transfer this mixture to the bowl with the livers.

Add the remaining butter to the pan and fry the ground nuts and breadcrumbs until lightly golden, then add the herbs.

SAUCE

100 ml (3½ fl oz/scant ½ cup) port
300 ml (10 fl oz/1¼ cups) fresh
  chicken stock
120 g (4 oz) cherries, pitted

KALE

200 g (7 oz) curly kale, chopped
3 tablespoons extra virgin
  olive oil
2 garlic cloves, finely sliced
lemon wedges, for squeezing

Transfer the mushroom and liver mixture to a small food processor and blitz together, adding a tablespoon of water if you need to, until it forms a smooth paste.

Mix this with the breadcrumbs and nuts and season. Divide this mixture between the partridge cavities, then place the partridges in a roasting tin (pan) and splash over a little more port.

Roast for 45 minutes until golden brown, then remove from the tin and set aside to rest.

Meanwhile, make the sauce. Place the roasting tin on the stove over a high heat and add the port. Bubble for a minute, then add the stock, along with any resting juices from the partridges. Bubble for a few minutes to intensify, then add the cherries and bubble for a minute more.

Blanch the kale in a pan of boiling water for 2–3 minutes, then drain. Heat the oil in a frying pan over a low heat, then add the kale and garlic and fry gently for 3–4 minutes. Season and add a squeeze of lemon, then serve with the partridges and sauce.

GRILLED RABBIT

Sometimes, all you need is a piece of good meat. I love the results you get by using natural cooking methods. A good meat, cooked simply and gently over the charcoals until it's crisp and golden on the outside and really juicy on the inside, with just a squeeze of lemon, makes me happy.

Rabbit is ideal for this style of cooking: it seems to lend itself well to the natural heat, and the true flavours intensify. It's actually a very healthy meat option, being very low in fat. Here, I've just grilled the meat over the coals without marinating it, but if you to add another flavour dimension, you can marinate the rabbit for a couple of hours using the same mix I suggested in the suckling pig recipe on page 134.

INGREDIENTS

1 x 1.2 kg (2 lb 10 oz) farmed
  rabbit, jointed into 8 pieces
2 tablespoons olive oil
extra virgin olive oil, for drizzling
sea salt and freshly ground
  black pepper
lemon halves seared on the
  barbecue, to serve

Prepare a barbecue with good-quality charcoal and light. Wait until it is really hot. Alternativelleny, heat a griddle pan over a high heat.

Place the rabbit legs and shoulder pieces on the barbecue or griddle pan. Cook for 20 minutes, turning occasionally, then add the saddle/rib pieces and cook for another 15–20 minutes, turning occasionally, until all the pieces are golden and cooked through.

Drizzle with extra virgin olive oil and season, then serve with lemon halves for squeezing over.

THE SPANISH HOME KITCHEN

CITRUS SALAD WITH CHORIZO AND CRISPY FRIED EGG

When I told friends about this recipe, they weren't very sure at all, but they love it now! Sometimes we see citrus fruits served with a boiled egg but not very often with a fried one. This recipe is from Las Hurdes, a really beautiful area in the north of Extremadura. It is often simply called *ensalada de naranja* – orange salad – which is a bit unfair on all the other ingredients, but they all work together to make a really great dish.

If you like, you can cook up more chorizo than the recipe says. After all, it's really addictive ...

INGREDIENTS

1 lemon
3 oranges
60 ml (2 fl oz/¼ cup) olive oil
100 g (3½ oz) fresh chorizo, diced
4 garlic cloves, sliced
2 free-range eggs
sea salt and freshly ground black pepper

TO SERVE

extra virgin olive oil
microherb leaves, such as amaranth, pea or radish
sourdough toast

Remove the peel from the citrus fruits and cut into segments. Arrange on plates.

Heat 2 tablespoons of the olive oil in a small frying pan (skillet) over a medium-high heat and fry the chorizo until golden and crisp. Remove the chorizo from the pan and set aside on a plate. Add the garlic to the pan and allow to cook for 1 minute more, then remove from the heat and set aside to allow the garlic flavour to infuse into the oil.

Heat the remaining oil in a non-stick frying pan over a high heat and fry the eggs for 2 minutes until the whites are a little golden and crisp, but the yolk is still runny. Spoon a little of the hot oil over the yolk to just set the top.

Place the eggs on top of the citrus fruits, then scatter over the chorizo and drizzle with the garlicky oil.

To serve, season with salt and pepper. Scatter over the microherbs and serve with toast. The best way to eat it is to cut up the eggs and mix everything together so that the yolk combines with the citrus and rich chorizo.

COCIDO

When I was living with my parents in Talaván, we would often have cocido on cold Sundays in the winter and late autumn. I love it so much that when I visit home now, my mum cooks it for me even when it's 40°C outside!

You need to take your time with this dish, both when cooking and eating. It's important to cook it low and slow, and then to take the time to eat first the soup, then the chickpeas, and then the meat.

You can cook the chorizo and the morcilla separately in order to make a clearer soup – that's how my mum does it – but I love the great flavour of the chorizo and morcilla in my soup!

COCIDO

250 g (9 oz) dried chickpeas
  soaked overnight in warm water
2 large carrots, peeled
2 onions, cut into thin wedges
1 large leek, chopped
2 chicken legs (500 g/1 lb 2 oz)
2 beef ribs (about 800 g/1 lb 12 oz)
4 pork belly strips (450 g/1 lb)
1 small ham hock (1 kg/2 lb 4 oz)
2 bay leaves
5 fresh thyme sprigs
200 g (7 oz) chorizo, sliced
200 g (7 oz) morcilla, roughly
  chopped
sea salt and freshly ground
  black pepper

SOUP

200 g (7 oz) small pasta shapes

CHICKPEA AND MEAT COURSES

250 g (9 oz) tomatoes, finely
  chopped
1 small onion, finely chopped
handful of flat-leaf parsley,
  chopped
3 tablespoons extra virgin
  olive oil
1 small savoy cabbage
2 tablespoons olive oil
2 garlic cloves, finely sliced
½ teaspoon sweet smoked
  pimentón de la Vera
2 teaspoons red wine vinegar

Begin by making the cocido. Drain the soaked chickpeas and put them in a large saucepan with the rest of the cocido ingredients, except the chorizo and morcilla. Cover with cold water (about 2–3 litres/70–100 fl oz/8½–12½ cups) and season well. Bring to the boil, then simmer for 4 hours until the meat is very tender and the stock very flavourful. Add the chorizo and morcilla for the last 40 minutes of cooking.

For the first course, cook the pasta in 1.5 litres (51 fl oz/ 6 cups) of the cocido stock for around 5 minutes (or according to the packet instructions) until tender, then serve.

For the second course, mix together the tomatoes, onion, half of the parsley and extra virgin olive oil to make a tomato salad. Shred the cabbage and blanch in boiling water for 5–6 minutes, then drain. Heat the oil in a pan and fry the garlic for 1 minute, then add the blanched cabbage and pimentón. Season and add the vinegar. Toss with the chickpeas from the cocido and a little splash of the stock.

For the final course, serve a little of each type of meat to each person. Scatter with the rest of the parsley. I also like to serve this with crusty bread.

PINCHOS MORUNOS

Ahh! Delicious pinchos. We love these in my family, and they're probably more popular in Extremadura and Andalusia than anywhere else, although you will find different versions throughout Spain. They're actually a remnant of Moorish cuisine, similar to kebabs, but I'm sure they would have marinated them in exotic spices, and of course used they would have used lamb. In Extremadura, we call them pinchitos, because we love the little things. At home, we always use good-quality pork for this dish, or sometimes free-range chicken. My preference is to use pork loin, but any good cut of high-quality meat will work.

        Don't try and be posh with this one. Eat it with fries and a tomato salad—it's devilishly good!

INGREDIENTS

2 teaspoons sweet smoked pimentón de la Vera
1 teaspoon dried oregano
½ teaspoon dried chilli (hot pepper) flakes
1 teaspoon ground cumin
1 tablespoon sherry vinegar
2 tablespoons olive oil
800 g (1 lb 12 oz) pork loin, cut into 2.5 cm (1 in) chunks
sea salt and freshly ground black pepper

PATATAS FRITAS

900 g (2 lb) floury potatoes, peeled and cut into chips (fries)
1 litre (34 fl oz/4 cups) vegetable or olive oil, for deep-frying
sea salt

In a small bowl, mix the pimentón, oregano, chilli and cumin with the vinegar and oil, season well and pour into a dish. Add the diced pork and toss well, then leave to marinate for at least 2 hours or, even better, overnight.

Prepare your barbecue with good-quality charcoal and light it.

Thread the meat on to metal skewers. For the *patatas fritas*, put the chips (fries) into a large pan of cold salted water and bring to the boil. Simmer for 2–3 minutes, then drain and return to the pan over a low heat to dry the potatoes. Pour the oil into a deep sauté pan: you want it to be about 4 cm (1½ in) deep. Heat the oil to 180°C (350°F), or until a cube of bread browns in 30 seconds. Add the potatoes and fry for 3–4 minutes until golden. Drain on a plate lined with paper towels and season with sea salt. Set aside, keeping them warm.

Meanwhile, barbecue the skewers for 5–6 minutes, turning every so often, until the meat is charred and tender. Serve with the *patatas fritas* and a simple tomato salad, if you like.

TIP

If you want to cook these indoors, they are super easy to cook on a griddle pan or under a hot grill (broiler). Just remember to turn regularly to get that nice charring on the meat.

LENTILS WITH CHORIZO AND POTATOES

This is my desert-island dish, without a doubt. During an interview at CarFest one year, I was asked what would be my 'death-row' dish. At first, I wasn't sure what the interviewer meant, but after a few moments I realised what I was being asked. The dish I chose was this one, and I stand by that choice today. Well, it would definitely have to be one of the many courses, anyway. This wasn't always the way – when I was a kid, I don't know why, but I couldn't stand lentils. I remember a big drama when I was a toddler: because I turned my nose up at lentils one lunchtime, I had to have them for dinner as well… and then again for breakfast the next day! To be fair, I was a 'challenging' child, and I know I must have been difficult. Anyway, back to now – I absolutely love lentils, and guess what? This dish is ideal for breakfast, lunch or dinner. My mum was right. It's perfect for all year round, too, so go ahead, enjoy!

INGREDIENTS

2 tablespoons olive oil
250 g (9 oz) chorizo, sliced
1 onion, finely sliced
2 garlic cloves, finely sliced
1 small carrot, chopped
300 g (10½ oz) large floury
    potatoes, quartered or cut
    into large chunks
1–2 fresh bay leaves
250 g (9 oz) puy lentils, rinsed
1 litre (34 fl oz/4 cups) fresh
    chicken stock
150 g (5 oz) morcilla, chopped
sea salt and freshly ground
    black pepper
crusty bread, to serve

Heat the olive oil in a deep casserole dish (Dutch oven) over a medium heat. Add the chorizo slices and cook until golden on both sides. Once cooked, remove from the pan with a slotted spoon and set aside on a plate, leaving the reddish oil in the pan.

Add the onion to the pan and cook for 5 minutes until slightly softened, then add the garlic and cook for a further minute or two. Add the carrot, potatoes and bay leaves to the pan and cook for another couple of minutes, stirring occasionally.

Add the lentils, followed by the stock. Season well and bring to the boil. Reduce to a simmer and cook, covered, for 30 minutes, or until the lentils have softened but still have some bite. The mixture should still be quite soupy; if it is a little too dry, add another splash of stock. Return the chorizo to the pan, along with the morcilla, and cook, uncovered, for 5–7 minutes. Serve in warmed bowls with crusty bread.

GOLDEN LAMB CUTLETS WITH LEMON COURGETTE SALAD

This is a favourite dish of my mum's – in fact, everyone at home loves it. Normally, you would just cook the cutlets on the grill or barbecue, but here I've fried them for a lovely, crispy finish.

These tasty cutlets are great for a picnic as they taste just as good cold, dipped in mayonnaise. We've used baby lamb here; if you use older lamb, you might prefer to trim off some of the fat. But, as I always say, in the fat is the flavour!

INGREDIENTS

2 x 6-rib French trimmed racks
    of spring lamb, sliced into
    cutlets (chops)
3 tablespoons olive oil, plus
    75 ml (2½ fl oz/5 tablespoons)
    for frying
finely grated zest and juice of
    1 lemon
3 lemon thyme sprigs
2 garlic cloves, bashed
2 teaspoons coriander seeds,
    bashed in a pestle and mortar
2 handfuls of plain
    (all-purpose) flour
2 free-range eggs, lightly beaten
sea salt and freshly ground
    black pepper

LEMON COURGETTE SALAD

4 courgettes (zucchini), thinly
    sliced lengthways
1 tablespoon olive oil
½ teaspoon dried chilli
    (hot pepper) flakes
200 g (7 oz) freshly shelled peas
200 g (7 oz) freshly shelled
    broad (fava) beans
juice of 1 lemon
handful mint leaves
4 tablespoons extra virgin
    olive oil
100 g (3½ oz) fresh cows' cheese
    (page 38), or you can use
    crumbled feta or crumbled
    goats' cheese

Arrange the lamb cutlets in a large dish. In a small bowl, combine the 3 tablespoons of olive oil with the lemon zest and juice, lemon thyme, garlic and coriander seeds. Pour this mixture over the lamb and season with plenty of freshly ground black pepper. Toss to coat and leave to marinate overnight in the fridge.

The next day, heat the 75 ml (2½ fl oz/5 tablespoons) oil in a large pan over a high heat until it shimmers. Remove the lamb from the marinade. Place the flour in a shallow bowl and season, and have the beaten eggs ready in a second bowl. Working in batches, dip the cutlets in the seasoned flour and then the egg, and then place them straight into the hot oil. Fry for 2–3 minutes, then turn and fry on the other side until golden brown. Set aside on a plate lined with paper towels and keep warm while you fry the remaining cutlets.

Meanwhile, make the salad. Toss the courgettes (zucchini) in a large bowl with the oil and chilli (hot pepper) flakes. Place a griddle pan over a high heat and sear the courgette slices on both sides, then tip into a serving bowl. Blanch the peas and broad (fava) beans in boiling water for 2–3 minutes, then drain and add to the serving bowl, along with the rest of the salad ingredients. Toss to combine, then season and serve with the golden lamb cutlets.

BRAISED PORK RIBS AND POTATOES WITH FRIED HERBY CRUMBS

El Día de la Matanza is the day that the lovely pigs pass on to a better life, providing food for the family for the whole year. In Spain we say *'Del cerdo se come hasta los andares'* – 'From the pig, we eat even the walking!' (I'm not sure quite how you are supposed to eat the 'walking' of the pig, but the idea is that it's all about using every part of the animal.) This recipe is always on the menu on el *Día de la Matanza*, and it was one of my dad's favourites.

    The way my mum makes it is quite simple: she just slow-cooks the ribs until really tender, and then she adds the potatoes – she doesn't include the crumbs. Both ways are delicious, but I think the crumb adds an extra something special.

INGREDIENTS

1.5–2 kg (3 lb 5 oz–4 lb 8 oz) baby back ribs
1 teaspoon pimentón de la Vera
4 garlic cloves, bashed
4 tablespoons olive oil
1½ teaspoons cumin seeds, lightly crushed
150 ml (5 fl oz/scant ⅔ cup) white wine
1 large onion, finely sliced
2 bay leaves
500 ml (17 fl oz/2 cups) fresh chicken stock
300 g (10½ oz) new potatoes

FRIED HERBY CRUMBS

4 tablespoons olive oil
1 garlic clove, finely grated
75 g (2½ oz) fresh white breadcrumbs
finely grated zest of 1 lemon
6 sage leaves, shredded

Arrange the ribs in a large dish. Add the pimentón, 2 of the grated garlic cloves, 2 tablespoons of the olive oil, 1 teaspoon of the crushed cumin seeds and 50 ml (1¾ fl oz/ 3 tablespoons) of the white wine and combine to coat the ribs. Leave to marinate for at least 3 hours, or overnight if you can, in the fridge.

Preheat the oven to 170°C/150°C fan/340°F/gas 3½.

Heat the remaining 2 tablespoons of olive oil in a deep casserole dish (Dutch oven) over a high heat. Remove the ribs from the marinade, then cook for 4–5 minutes on each side until browned all over. Set the ribs aside on a plate and add the onion to the pan. Cook for 10 minutes until brown, then add the remaining garlic cloves and cumin seeds. Stir to combine, then return the ribs to the pan.

Pour in the remaining white wine and bubble for a minute, then add the bay leaves and stock, along with the leftover marinade. Season well and bring to the boil, then cover and transfer to the oven to cook for 1–1½ hours, until the meat has softened and is beginning to pull away from the bone.

Crack the new potatoes in half with the tip of a knife (this helps them release the starch) then add to the casserole dish and cook for a further 30–40 minutes, or until the potatoes are tender and starting to break apart and thicken the sauce.

Meanwhile, prepare the herby crumbs. Heat the oil in
a frying pan (skillet) over a medium high heat and fry the
garlic for 10 seconds, then add the breadcrumbs, lemon
zest and sage.

Remove the lid from the casserole dish and sprinkle this
crumb all over the top, then cook uncovered for a further
20 minutes and serve in shallow bowls with lots of the lovely
sauce from the dish.

MEAT

SHOULDER OF IBERICO PORK IN RICH TOMATO SAUCE WITH LEMONY COUSCOUS

Fresh Ibérico meat is becoming very popular now in the UK, but this wasn't the case not so long ago. I still remember the first time I put this meat on the menu at Eyre Brothers restaurant – I think it was in around 2002. Initially, David wasn't sure about serving pork rare or medium-rare, but after I proved to him all was safe, he agreed, and he kept the dish on the menu for a very long time.

This recipe, though, is not rare at all! In fact, it is cooked for several hours, which makes the meat so tender and tasty. Couscous is a favourite in our home, and I have to say Peter is a master at it!

INGREDIENTS

2 tablespoons olive oil
1.5 kg (3 lb 5 oz) shoulder of Iberico pork, cut into 5 cm (2 in) chunks
2 red onions, finely sliced
3 garlic cloves, finely sliced
2 teaspoons coriander seeds, lightly bashed
1 tablespoon tomato purée (paste)
150 ml (5 fl oz/scant ⅔ cup) oloroso sherry
400 g (14 oz) tin chopped tomatoes
400 ml (13 fl oz/generous 1½ cups) fresh chicken stock
sea salt and freshly ground black pepper

Preheat the oven to 160°C/140°C fan/325°F/gas 3.

Heat the oil in a large casserole dish (Dutch oven) over a medium-high heat. Season the pork all over and cook for 5–6 minutes until browned, working in batches. Once each batch is cooked, remove with tongs and set aside on a plate. Every so often, pour off the fat that renders from the meat. Keep this for frying another time, as it has amazing flavour.

Once all the pork is cooked, decrease the heat to medium low and add the onions to the casserole dish and gently fry for 10 minutes, then add the garlic and coriander seeds and fry for 5 minutes more.

Add the tomato purée and sherry and bubble for 1 minute, then return the pork to the pan and add the tinned tomatoes and stock. Season and bring to a simmer, then cover and transfer to the oven. Cook for 2½–3 hours until the meat is really tender.

Meanwhile, prepare the couscous. First put the red onion in a heatproof bowl. Pour over some boiling water from the kettle and leave to sit for 30 seconds, then drain using a colander. Cool under cool running water.

Tip the onion back into the bowl and squeeze over the lemon juice. Season with sea salt and set aside.

LEMONY COUSCOUS

1 red onion, finely sliced
juice of 1 lemon
250 g (9 oz/1⅓ cups) couscous
3 tablespoons extra virgin
  olive oil
450 ml (15 fl oz/1¾ cups) hot
  chicken stock
large handful of flat-leaf parsley,
  chopped, plus extra to serve
2 preserved lemons, skin finely
  sliced
½ cucumber, peeled, deseeded
  and finely diced
30 g (1½ oz) toasted flaked
  (slivered) almonds

Put the couscous in a flat dish. Stir in the extra virgin olive oil and a good pinch of sea salt, then pour over the hot chicken stock. Stir and cover with cling film (plastic wrap), then leave to stand for 10 minutes. Remove the cling film and fluff the couscous with a fork. Add the remaining ingredients and stir.

Serve the pork with the couscous, the pickled onion and its juices and another scattering of parsley.

THE SPANISH HOME KITCHEN

MIGAS WITH FRIED EGG, CHORIZO AND BACON

Whenever I eat or cook this recipe, it takes me back to one of my earliest memories: my grandfather watching the evening news while cutting stale bread for making migas the next day. Migas was traditionally eaten almost every day, as it was great fuel for people working on the farms. It's certainly not low in calories – but then nothing good is!

There are so many different ways to prepare migas. Back at home, my family use just olive oil to cook the garlic and bread, and then cook the meat separately, serving it with a *café con leche*. I like to cook the chorizo first and then stir it back in at the end – and I love it with a great glass of red wine.

INGREDIENTS

250 g (9 oz) stale crusty bread, torn into large chunks
125 ml (4¼ fl oz/½ cup) water
100 ml (3½ fl oz/scant ½ cup) olive oil
120 g (4 oz) chorizo, diced
3 garlic cloves, bashed
4 thick slices of streaky bacon (each slice a good 1 cm/ ½ in thick)
4 free-range eggs
sea salt

Put the stale bread chunks in a dish and sprinkle with 50 ml (1¾ fl oz/3 tablespoons) of the water. Cover with a damp tea towel and leave for at least 3 hours (or overnight).

Heat the oil in a large pan over a medium heat and gently fry the chorizo and garlic for 2–3 minutes until the chorizo is golden. Remove with a slotted spoon and set aside on a plate.

Add the rest of the water to the pan along with a generous pinch of salt. Add a handful of the bread and mix really well, then add the rest of the bread to the pan and increase the heat to medium heat. Cook, stirring occasionally, for 15 minutes, until the chunks of bread are golden and crisp but still tender in the middle.

Meanwhile, in a separate non-stick pan, fry the bacon slices over a medium-high heat for 3–5 minutes until golden and crisp, then remove and set aside with the chorizo.

Keeping the pan on the heat, crack in the eggs and fry them in the bacon fat until they are done to your liking.

Once golden, stir the chorizo and garlic back into the *migas* (the bread chunks). Serve with the bacon and eggs.

MOORISH MEATBALLS

WITH SPINACH, PINE NUTS AND SPICED SAFFRON YOGHURT

Meatballs are one of my favourite things to cook. They're a great way to play around with different flavours – in my previous books and my restaurant menus, I've experimented with meatballs made of everything from squid to salt cod, served with sauces made from almonds, oranges, tomatoes and more.

This recipe is very quick, and really different to any meatball dishes I've made before. It's perfect for a midweek supper or tapas evening.

INGREDIENTS

2 tablespoons olive oil
1 banana shallot, finely chopped
300 g (10½ oz) beef mince (ground beef)
300 g (10½ oz) pork mince (ground pork)
2 fat garlic cloves, grated
1 teaspoon hot smoked pimentón de la Vera
1 teaspoon sweet smoked pimentón de la Vera
1 teaspoon ground cumin
handful of chopped coriander (cilantro), plus extra to garnish
30 g (1 oz) pine nuts, toasted
250 g (9 oz) baby spinach
30 g (1 oz) sultanas
sea salt and freshly ground black pepper
crusty bread, to serve

SPICED SAFFRON YOGHURT

300 g (10½ oz) Greek yoghurt
1 garlic clove, grated
1 tablespoon finely chopped mint leaves
pinch of saffron threads, soaked in 1 teaspoon boiling water
1 tablespoon extra virgin olive oil

Preheat the oven to 180°C/160°C fan/350°F/gas 4. Heat 1 tablespoon of the oil in a small frying pan (skillet) over a low heat and gently fry the shallot for 10 minutes until soft. Set aside and allow to cool.

In a large bowl, mix together both types of mince, along with the garlic, cooled shallot, spices and chopped coriander. Season well and shape into 16 walnut-sized balls.

Heat the remaining oil in a large ovenproof frying pan over a medium–high heat. Add the meatballs and fry until they are golden, then transfer to the oven for 5 minutes to finish cooking. Remove to a warm plate and cover loosely with kitchen foil.

Meanwhile, make the spiced saffron yoghurt. In a bowl, mix together the yoghurt, garlic and mint and season well, then stir in the saffron and its soaking water.

Place the frying pan you used for the meatballs over a high heat and add the spinach and sultanas, along with a small splash of water. Mix together and allow the spinach to wilt and mingle with the cooking juices from the meatballs. Add the pine nuts, then return the meatballs and any resting juices back into the pan and toss everything together.

Divide the yoghurt between 4 plates and top with the meatballs and spinach. Serve with crusty bread.

BARBECUED SHOULDER OF LAMB WITH OLIVE AND HERB CRUST

AND ESCALIVADA AND POTATO PARCEL

Barbecuing seems to be more popular than ever before, and it's not just for summer. We are learning how important it is to spend time outdoors and be with our family and friends – and there's no better way to do that than cooking.

Cooking on a barbecue often makes me think about the way humans first started to cook over fire. I like to think someone was just looking at the fire one day and thought, 'How much better would it be to put the food on there?' I'm sure there are studies to read about how it happened, but I just want to thank whoever came up with the idea – because it is one of the best joys in life!

INGREDIENTS

175 g (6 oz) pitted green olives
finely grated zest of 1 lemon
3 garlic cloves
5 cured anchovies
large handful of flat-leaf parsley
5 lemon thyme sprigs, leaves
   picked
small handful of
   fresh mint
6 tablespoons olive oil
2–2.2 kg (4 lb 8 oz–5 lb 8 oz)
   lamb shoulder, boned
sea salt and freshly ground
   black pepper

ESCALIVADA AND POTATO PARCEL

900 g (2 lb) new potatoes,
   thickly sliced
1 red onion, cut into thin wedges
190g (6½ oz) roasted red
   peppers from a jar
2 aubergines (eggplants), cut
   into small cubes
6 tablespoons extra virgin
   olive oil
1 tablespoon sherry vinegar
2 tablespoons chopped chives

Put the olives, lemon zest, garlic, anchovies, herbs and olive oil in a food processor and pulse to form a paste. Season well. Spread all over the inside and outside of the lamb shoulder and set aside while you light the barbecue.

Light your coals and set up the barbecue for indirect cooking (this means the coals are on either side of the barbecue, leaving the middle free). Place a drip tray in the centre of the barbecue below the grill, between the two areas of coals, to catch the fat. You want an initial temperature of about 200–220°C (400–425°F), which will then drop to about 170°C (340°F). You need enough coals for a good couple of hours' cooking at about 170°C (340°F).

Place the lamb in the centre of the barbecue on the grill. Cover and cook for 1½–2 hours, allowing the temperature to drop as described above.

Meanwhile, arrange two large pieces of kitchen foil on a work surface in a cross shape. Pile all the potato parcel ingredients, except the chives, into the centre and season well. Bring up the sides up to form a parcel.

After the lamb has cooked for an hour or so, put the parcel next to it over some of the hot coals. Cover the barbecue once more and continue cooking.

Once the lamb is tender, remove it from the barbecue and rest for at least 10 minutes. Open the potato parcel and scatter with chives, then serve with the lamb.

SEARED VEAL RIB

WITH FRIED POTATOES, MOJO ROJO AND LEMON THYME MAYO

In my family, veal was more popular than beef, and often the meat we had was from our own animals. My dad would often say, 'We know this meat is from happy animals.' In Spain, veal is produced by keeping the calves with their mothers until they are five to six months old, then feeding them with grass and cereals until they are nine months old – and around 400 kg (880 lb)!

Veal isn't so popular in the UK as it hasn't got the best reputation, but if you find a local butcher you can trust, they can help you get a great, happy meat. The two sauces here are great with the veal, but also go brilliantly with any other meat, as well as fish or grilled vegetables.

LEMON THYME MAYO

250 ml (8½ fl oz/1 cup) olive oil
4 lemon thyme sprigs
2 egg yolks
2 teaspoons white wine vinegar
50 ml (1¾ fl oz/3 tablespoons)
  extra virgin olive oil
lemon juice, to taste

VEAL AND POTATOES

1 kg (2 lb 4 oz) floury potatoes,
  diced
1 large rib (or 2 smaller ribs) of
  rose veal côte de veau (about
  800 g/1 lb 12 oz), at room
  temperature
100 ml (3½ fl oz/scant ½ cup)
  olive oil, plus extra for rubbing
sea salt and freshly ground
  black pepper

MOJO ROJO SAUCE

150 g (5 oz) piquillo or roasted
  red peppers
2 teaspoons choricero
  pepper paste
1 garlic clove, grated
½ teaspoon ground cumin
½ teaspoon pimenton de la Vera
2–3 tablespoons extra virgin
  olive oil
2 teaspoons apple vinegar

Put the olive oil and lemon thyme for the mayo in a small saucepan over a low heat. Heat gently for 2–3 minutes, then take off the heat and set aside to infuse for half an hour or more.

Preheat the oven to 220°C/200°C fan/425°F/gas 7.

Put the potatoes in a pan of cold salted water and bring to the boil. Simmer for a couple of minutes, then drain and return to the pan over a low heat to dry and fluff up.

Meanwhile, make the *mojo rojo* sauce and mayo. For the *mojo rojo*, blitz all the ingredients together and season well.

For the mayo, beat the egg yolks and white wine vinegar with plenty of seasoning. Gradually whisk in the infused oil, followed by the extra virgin, until you have a thick mayonnaise. Add a splash of hot water to loosen, then stir in the lemon to taste..

Rub the veal with oil and season well. Heat a heavy-based frying pan (skillet) over a high heat and sear the veal for 2–3 minutes on each side, then transfer to a roasting tin (pan) and roast in the oven for 10–12 minutes. Set aside to rest for 10 minutes.

Heat the 100 ml (3½ fl oz/scant ½ cup) oil in a heavy-based frying pan over a high heat and fry the potatoes for 10–12 minutes, turning until really golden and crisp all over. Add the capers for the last minute so they become crispy too. Drain both on a plate lined with paper towels and season well.

Remove the rib bone from the veal and slice. Serve with the crispy potatoes, *mojo rojo* sauce and lemon thyme mayo.

Choricero peppers are large, mild, fleshy red peppers that have a lovely sweet and earthy flavour. They are dried and turned into a paste for adding richness and depth to dishes.

MUSHROOM- AND TRUFFLE-STUFFED SPATCHCOCK CHICKEN

In Talaván, we have a type of white truffle called criadilla de tierra (it can't really be translated, but it roughly means 'growing from the earth'). It's not as aromatic as other truffles and is a bit softer in texture. We love them, and the most popular way we serve them is in a tortilla with some caramelised onions – just beautiful – or in a stew with potatoes and chicken. This recipe has all those flavours, just put together in a different way. ¡Salud!

INGREDIENTS

800 g (1 lb 12 oz) floury potatoes, cut into chunks
4 tablespoons olive oil
1 large garlic clove, grated
150 g (5 oz) mushrooms, finely chopped
4 pancetta rashers, very finely sliced
7 g (¼ oz) fresh black truffle, shaved (I used 1 truffle)
2 heaped tablespoons soft/cream cheese
1 tablespoon finely chopped flat-leaf parsley
1 large free-range chicken (about 2 kg/4 lb 8 oz), spatchcocked (see Tip)
3 parsnips, sliced lengthways
3 carrots, sliced lengthways
a few fresh thyme sprigs, leaves picked
sea salt and freshly ground black pepper

Preheat the oven to 220°C/200°C fan/425°F/gas 7.

Put the potatoes in a large saucepan of cold salted water and bring to the boil, then reduce the heat to low and simmer for 5 minutes until the edges of the potatoes are tender. Drain and return to the pan to fluff up over a low heat. Set aside.

Heat half the oil in a frying pan (skillet) over a medium-high heat and fry the garlic and mushrooms for 5 minutes until the mushrooms are golden. Tip into a bowl and set aside to cool. Add the pancetta, truffle, soft cheese and parsley to the bowl and mix everything together. Season well.

Use your fingers to release the skin over the breast of the chicken and spread the mushroom-and-truffle mixture over the flesh underneath.

Toss the potatoes in a roasting tin (pan) with the parsnips, carrots and thyme, and drizzle with the remaining oil.

Place the chicken on a roasting rack with the roasting tin of vegetables underneath to catch the juices and fat as the meat roasts. Roast for 20 minutes, then reduce the heat to 180°C/160°C fan/350°F/gas 4 and roast for a further 40 minutes, tossing the vegetables every so often until they are golden and crispy.

Let the chicken rest for 10 minutes, then when everything is ready, carve the chicken and serve with the roasted vegetables.

TIP

To spatchcock your chicken, place on a board, breast-side down.
Use a pair of poultry shears or sturdy scissors to cut along either
side of the parson's nose along the backbone so that you can
remove it. Turn it breast side up and using your hands, press down
hard along the breastbone until you feel it give and the bird
flattens out.

WARM BEEF, PIQUILLO PEPPER AND CHARRED ASPARAGUS SALAD

I call this an 'anytime salad'. Of course, you can't have asparagus in October, but it's a really versatile dish and you can just substitute it for whatever vegetables are in season. Whatever you use, I have to say it looks impressive on the table! It has great flavours and textures, but it is very important to eat as soon as is plated – if you let it sit too long, the salad might start to look a bit sad.

INGREDIENTS

2 ribeye steaks (about 250 g/ 9 oz each)
1 tablespoon olive oil
16 asparagus spears
2 baby gem lettuces, leaves separated
100 g (3½ oz) roasted piquillo peppers, sliced
2 tablespoons capers (baby capers)
30 g (1 oz) flaked (slivered) almonds, toasted
sea salt and freshly ground black pepper

DRESSING

1 garlic clove, grated
2–3 sprigs marjoram or oregano, leaves picked
2 tablespoons PX sherry vinegar
3–4 tablespoons extra virgin olive oil

Season the steaks and rub all over with oil. Heat a griddle pan over a high heat and, once hot, add the steaks. Griddle for 2–3 minutes on each side, then remove from the pan and set aside on a plate to rest.

Coat the asparagus spears with oil and add them to the hot griddle pan. Cook for 2–3 minutes, turning, until charred and blackened. Tip into a serving bowl.

Add the lettuce leaves, piquillo peppers and capers to the bowl with the asparagus.

To make the dressing, combine all the ingredients in a small jug or bowl and season well.

Slice the steaks and arrange on top of the salad, then drizzle all over with the dressing. Scatter over the toasted flaked almonds and serve.

SWEET

In Spain, or at least in my family, sweet things are mainly made at times of celebration. The Spanish palate is arguably more savoury than here in the UK, although there are some people who really love their sweet things. This may be due to the climate because people do tend to crave sweet things when it's colder, or maybe it's just the different food culture. Personally, I always prefer a plate of cheese followed by some dark chocolate after dinner, rather than a big pudding. I like to think it's because, as I often say, "I'm sweet enough" - but that's for you to decide! Peter, my partner, LOVES sweet things. We often call him *goloso* (a person who loves to eat sweets all the time). I think he got this from his mum, Hilda. She was also very *golosa* and an amazing baker. She made the best Victoria sponges and chocolate cakes. I notice in the restaurant too that some people just always look forward to the dessert dish, whilst others would much rather have some cheese … and some more wine, of course.

It was always so nice when my mum Isabel did cook sweet things at home. She would normally make things using the intense and aromatic honey from my dad's bees, that he kept in the vegetable plots. I remember her making Coquillos (featured in this chapter) and recall how much I loved the smell of hot honey and sweetness wafting through air, filling the whole house. This would make my mouth water, and be off to investigate. The recipes you'll see in this chapter are some of the top favourite sweet things that I remember family and friends making when I was growing up. Of course, I've also featured Peter's Almond Cake – a cake I really love, so this is on the menu in all my restaurants, and it's a firm favourite.

NATILLAS

Food in the roadside restaurants and bars in Spain is often really great – certainly not the same kind of thing as we usually get at service stations in the UK. In Spain, you really can find great places to eat and relax on long trips, getting a good-quality (and great-value) menu del día. One thing you'll often find is natillas, a creamy custard dish served with biscuits on top. It always makes me happy, because it reminds me of opening the fridge at home and being excited to see we had natillas. Here, we will make our own biscuits. In Spain, we use galletas María rather than butter biscuits, but these work just as well. This recipe makes more biscuits that you'll need, but they keep very well in an airtight container, and are delicious when enjoyed with that classic British institution, the cup of tea.

BISCUITS (COOKIES)

275 g (10 oz/1¼ cups) plain (all-purpose) flour
1 teaspoon baking powder
good pinch of salt
80 g (3 oz/⅓ cup) caster (superfine) sugar
50 g (2 oz) unsalted butter, chilled and cubed
75 ml (2½ fl oz/1/3 cup) cold full-fat (whole) milk

CUSTARD

400 ml (13 fl oz/generous 1½ cups) full-fat (whole) milk
200 ml (7 fl oz/scant 1 cup) double (heavy) cream
1 cinnamon stick
pared zest of 1 lemon
3 free-range egg yolks
3 tablespoons caster (superfine) sugar, plus extra to serve
1 tablespoon cornflour (cornstarch)
toasted flaked (slivered) almonds, to serve
ground cinnamon, for dusting

Preheat the oven to 210°C/190°C fan/410°F/gas 6½ and line a baking sheet with baking parchment. Begin by making the biscuits. Mix together the flour, baking powder, salt and sugar in a bowl, then add the cold butter and rub together with your fingertips to incorporate it into the dry mixture.

Add the milk slowly and bring together into a dough. Knead briefly until smooth, then roll out on a lightly floured surface to a thickness of 2–3 mm Use a 6 cm (2½ in) round cutter to cut out biscuits and lift on to the prepared baking sheet. Use a fork to prick the biscuits all over, then bake for 12-15 minutes. Cool on the tray for 1 minute, then transfer to a wire rack to cool completely.

Meanwhile, combine the milk and cream in a pan over a medium heat. Add the cinnamon and zest and bring nearly to the boil, take off the heat then infuse for 20 minutes.

In a bowl, beat together the egg yolks, sugar and cornflour (cornstarch). Strain the warm milk mixture over the top, then whisk everything together.

Pour the mixture into a clean pan over a medium heat. Cook, stirring, until you have a really thick, glossy custard. Pour into 6 small dishes and then press a biscuit into the top of each. Chill for at least 3 hours before serving with a scattering of almonds and a dusting of cinnamon and sugar.

CHERRIES IN AGUARDIENTE SYRUP WITH PISTACHIO ICE CREAM

I recently got some samples of pistachios from a supplier in Spain – they were really good quality, amazing in fact. The cherries we produce in Spain are also exceptional – especially those grown in Extremadura, which is one of the best places in the world for a particular type of cherry called Picota. They are named for their peaked shape, and they naturally separate from their stalks when picked. They are a true jewel in the crown of my home region. My dad used to love cherries. I remember him getting into trouble with my mum if he had cherry stains around his mouth – evidence that he'd been eating too much before lunch or dinner!

INGREDIENTS

600 g (1 lb 5 oz) ripe cherries
200 g (7 oz/scant 1 cup) caster (superfine) sugar
200 ml (7 fl oz/scant 1 cup) water
150 ml (5 fl oz/scant ⅔ cup) aguardiente

PISTACHIO ICE CREAM

200 g (7 oz) shelled pistachios
150 g (5 oz/⅔ cup) caster (superfine) sugar
600 ml (20 fl oz/2 ½ cups) full-fat (whole) milk
6 free-range egg yolks
300 ml (10 fl oz/1¼ cups) double (heavy) cream
40 g (1½ oz) nibbed pistachios

To prepare the cherries, remove the stalks and pierce each cherry once with a cocktail stick (toothpick). Put the sugar and water in a saucepan over a low heat for 3–5 minutes until it melts. Bring up to a simmer and bubble until you have a thick, syrupy mixture.

Add the cherries and cook for a couple of minutes.

Strain the cherries and put them into jars. Allow the syrup to cool, then add the aguardiente. Stir to combine, then pour this syrup over the cherries and seal the jars. Allow to macerate for at least a month – but the longer, the better.

To make the ice cream, whizz the shelled pistachios in a food processor with half the sugar until you have a fine powder.

Heat the milk in a saucepan with the pistachio mixture over a medium-high heat until almost boiling. Remove from the heat and let infuse for at least 1 hour, and up to 4 hours. Beat the egg yolks with the remaining sugar until light and fluffy.

Pour the milk and pistachios into a sieve (fine mesh strainer) lined with muslin (cheesecloth) over a bowl. Squeeze out as much of the liquid as you can into the bowl, then gradually pour the pistachio milk over the eggs and mix well.

Return the mixture to the pan and cook over a medium heat for 15 minutes or so, until you have a very thick custard that coats the back of a spoon.

Strain into a bowl or jug (pitcher) and chill completely for a few hours. Add the double cream and nibbed pistachios to this chilled mixture, then pour into an ice-cream maker and churn until set. Scoop into a lidded container and freeze.

When the cherries have been soaking in the syrup a good while, you can serve them with scoops of the pistachio ice cream.

CARDAMOM AND ORANGE REPÁPALOS

Repápalos are always to be found on Isabel's menu at home at Easter time. My sister Isabel makes them really well too. She has practised the technique over the years and now has a real knack. I notice she always infuses the milk with cinnamon and orange peel, while being careful to never give flavours to the breadcrumbs. I'm bringing a different combination of flavours to this recipe: I just love the strength of cardamom and vanilla together. My sister – and my brother – would say to serve it hot, but I actually like it cold. However you serve it, this dessert is a winner.

INGREDIENTS

4 free-range eggs
1 teaspoon vanilla extract
100 g (3½ oz) fresh white
  breadcrumbs
75 g (2½ oz/⅓ cup) caster
  (superfine) sugar, plus extra
  for dusting
1 litre (34 fl oz/4 cups) olive oil,
  for deep-frying

SPICED MILK

300 ml (10 fl oz/1¼ cups)
  full-fat (whole) milk
3 cardamom pods
pared zest of 1 orange

In a bowl, beat together the eggs, vanilla, breadcrumbs and sugar to make a batter. Set aside for 30 minutes.

To prepare the spiced milk, pour the milk into a saucepan over a medium heat. Add the cardamom and orange zest and warm through for 5 minutes, then set aside to infuse.

Pour the oil for deep frying in a large saucepan over a medium-high heat. Heat the oil to 180°C (350°F), or if you don't have a thermometer, heat until a cube of bread browns in 20–25 seconds. Once the oil is hot, drop in dollops (around 2 tablespoons) of the batter and fry for 3–4 minutes on each side until golden brown. Set aside on a plate lined with paper towels while you fry the rest.

Strain the milk and warm through once more. Serve the golden *repápalos* bathed in the spiced milk and dusted in extra sugar.

THE SPANISH HOME KITCHEN

COQUILLOS WITH LAVENDER HONEY SYRUP

Coquillos, or pestiños to people in different parts of Spain, are a rich and devilishly sweet treat that my grandmother would make for special occasions. Our neighbour Dioni, who was always busy in her kitchen, would sometimes bring these over to the house for us to enjoy too. My mum would use dried lavender as a natural air freshener, or she'd make lavender bags to put in the wardrobe or to pop under the pillow, but she never added any lavender to the honey when she was making coquillos. Mark my words, though, with the addition of a little lavender, we are taking this dish to a different level!

INGREDIENTS

125 ml (4¼ fl oz/½ cup) extra virgin olive oil
pared zest of 1 orange
pared zest of 1 lemon
2 star anise
1 tablespoon caster (superfine) sugar
300 g (10½ oz/2½ cups) strong white flour, plus extra for dusting
1 teaspoon ground cinnamon
pinch of salt
125 ml (4¼ fl oz/½ cup) sweet wine
750 ml (25 fl oz/3 cups) vegetable oil, for deep-frying

HONEY SYRUP

175 g (6 oz/½ cup) honey
3 fresh lavender sprigs
2 tablespoons water

Pour the extra virgin olive oil into a small saucepan. Add the orange and lemon zest and warm for 1-2 minutes over a low heat, then remove from the heat and add the star anise. Set aside for 20 minutes, then strain the oil and set aside, reserving the star anise.

Place the star anise in a pestle and mortar with the sugar and crush to a paste.

In a mixing bowl, mix together the flour, cinnamon and salt. then add the infused oil and the star anise paste. Work together with your hands, adding the sweet wine as you go, until you have a soft dough.

Turn the dough out on to a lightly floured surface and knead for 10 minutes, then place in a clean bowl and cover with a damp tea towel. Leave to rest for 30 minutes to 1 hour at room temperature.

Place the syrup ingredients in a small saucepan over a medium heat. Warm through for 5 minutes, then set aside.

Pour the oil for deep-frying into a saucepan over a medium-high heat. Heat the oil to 170°C (340°F), or until a cube of bread browns in 40 seconds.

Working in batches, take small balls of the dough (about 20 g/¾ oz each) and roll each one out into a thin round. Press the opposite sides together in the middle and immediately fry in the oil for 2–3 minutes. Set aside on a plate lined with paper towels while you make the rest.

Bathe each coquillo in the lavender honey syrup, then shake off any excess and serve.

ARROPE

I don't have a big 'sweet tooth' and normally prefer cheese to finish a meal, but this is my type of dessert – even though it is actually very, very sweet. Maybe it's because it's ideal to serve with cheese. My partner Peter, however, does have a sweet tooth, and he always says he has two stomachs – one for savoury and one for sweet. He always has room for sweet things, just like his mum Hilda did. She would have loved this. In my region of Spain, this *arrope* is traditionally made with pumpkin, and would be used as candy. I used to get a piece from my grandmother when I was a good boy – not that it happened very often! In this recipe, I use different fruits, bringing them all together in a great combination of flavours and textures.

INGREDIENTS

1 litre (34 fl oz/4 cups) red grape juice
1 litre (34 fl oz/4 cups) white grape juice
150 g (5 oz/⅔ cup) caster (superfine) sugar
1 cinnamon stick
350 g (12 oz) chopped pumpkin or butternut squash
400 g (14 oz) just-ripe but still firm melon (piel de sapo, if you can find one, or honeydew), chopped
3 just-ripe figs, whole or halved
2 firm peaches, peeled, stoned and quartered

Mix together the grape juices in a large preserving pan over a high heat. Bring to the boil and reduce by nearly half. Add the sugar and cinnamon stick. Once the sugar has dissolved, add the pumpkin or squash, melon, figs and peaches.

Reduce the heat and simmer very gently for 1 hour, uncovered, until the fruit is very tender but not falling apart. Remove the fruit with a slotted spoon and place in a serving bowl. Increase the heat to high and let the liquid bubble and reduce until you have a thick, rich, sticky syrup. Pour this syrup over the fruit and allow to cool to room temperature, then chill for 1 hour before serving

HONEY ICE CREAM

Not all of life's experiences are joyful – some can bee (!) not so pleasant. I say this because I have a few memories of being stung by bees over the years – probably my own fault, trying to get into the beehives to get at the honey. I was a naughty boy – don't do it!

My dad always had bees on the farm. Honey in Extremadura is phenomenal due to our local flora and fauna. Honey is an essential ingredient in my home, and it's very important for me to have good-quality honey for my cooking. It goes without saying now that we need the bees for survival, so please try to buy from responsible local suppliers or from people you really trust. Talking about honey, on the next page you will see a picture of floretas, one of my favourite sweets. Dioni always makes them for me when I visit her – the recipe will be in my next book!

INGREDIENTS

300 ml (10 fl oz/1¼ cups)
   full-fat (whole) milk
good grating of fresh nutmeg
150 g (5 oz) flowery honey
6 free-range egg yolks
600 ml (20 fl oz/2½ cups)
   double (heavy) cream

Pour the milk into a saucepan over a medium-high heat. Add the nutmeg and honey and mix together. Warm through until almost boiling, then take off the heat.

Beat the egg yolks in a bowl and add to the pan with the hot milk. Mix together, then pour into a clean saucepan and cook over a medium heat, stirring, for 10 minutes until you have a glorious thick custard. Allow to cool, then chill until good and cold.

Add the cream to the cold honey custard. Pour into an ice-cream maker and churn until firm. Spoon into a tub with a lid and freeze for at least 3 hours before serving.

THE SPANISH HOME KITCHEN

MACEDONIA DE FRUTAS TROPICALES

This recipe is all about making a great syrup, because I know you don't need a recipe for fruit salad! At home in London, we have a lovely lemon verbena plant in the garden and we use it a lot in different dishes. I think you're going to love this syrup. It's just so yummy. It's funny that people often don't think mango, kiwi and pineapple are typically Spanish, but think again – these are very popular in Spain and grow well in the southern regions, and kiwis are always winners in Extremadura! Some of the best of these fruits are from my region.

SYRUP

75 g (2 ½ oz/scant ⅓ cup)
   caster (superfine) sugar
100 g (3½ oz/generous ¼ cup)
   honey
juice of 3 limes
a few lemon verbena or lemon
thyme sprigs

FRUIT

1 large, ripe mango, peeled
   and sliced
3 peaches, stoned and sliced
2 golden kiwi fruits, peeled
   and sliced
1 small ripe pineapple, skin and
   core removed, flesh sliced
2 blush or blood oranges,
   peeled and sliced

To make the syrup, put the sugar and honey in a small saucepan with the lime juice, herbs and a splash of water. Place over a low heat and allow the sugar to melt, then bubble for 10–12 minutes until you have a sticky but colourless syrup.

Arrange the fruit on a platter and drizzle with the syrup. Leave to macerate for 20–30 minutes, then serve.

TARTA DE MANZANA CASERA

I'm telling you, when Peter is not happy about something, you will know, and he was not very happy with an earlier version of this recipe. Okay, he said it was amazing, but asked me if I could improve on it. Anyway, after some tweaks here and there, and more tasting, he is happy – and, as you may know, he has a great palate. This is gorgeous recipe, perfect for when you are entertaining and looking for something a little more special than a normal apple tart. This one is thicker – and it's rich. You can prepare it a couple days before you want to serve it, and personally, I think it tastes better that way. Please try it with the pistachio ice-cream one page 192 for another match made in heaven!

INGREDIENTS

butter, for greasing
7 golden delicious apples, peeled, 5 cored and chopped and 2 thinly sliced
3 free-range eggs
100 g (3½ oz/scant ½ cup) caster (superfine) sugar, plus extra for sprinkling
150 ml (5 fl oz/scant ⅔ cup) full-fat milk
finely grated zest and juice of 1 lemon
200 g (7 oz/ generous 1½ cups) plain (all-purpose) flour
1 x 7 g (¼ oz) sachet fast action dried yeast
3 tablespoons apricot jam
2 tablespoons boiling water

Preheat the oven to 190°C/170°C fan/375°F/gas 5 and grease and line a 20 cm (8 in) springform cake tin.

Place the chopped apples in a blender with the eggs, sugar, milk and lemon zest and juice. Whizz together until you have a smooth batter. Pour into a bowl.

Sift the flour over the top and gently fold in, then stir in the yeast. Leave to stand for 45 minutes–1 hour at room temperature to allow the yeast to start to work. The batter will bubble a bit and expand a little.

Pour the mixture into the tin and bake for 20 minutes.

Remove from the oven and arrange the thinly sliced apple over the top of the cake. Sprinkle over some sugar, then return the cake to the oven and cook for 20–30 minutes more until the cake is cooked through and a skewer inserted into the middle comes out clean.

Melt the jam in a small saucepan with the boiling water over a medium heat. Sieve well, then brush all over the apples on top of the cake while they are still warm. Cool in the tin for 10 minutes, then transfer to a wire rack to cool completely. It will keep in an airtight container for 4–5 days.

TÉCULA-MÉCULA

This recipe originates from the time of the Berber-Hispanic Muslims in Spain, and this is very clear from the ingredients we use. *Técula-mécula* means 'for you, for me', and it's very popular throughout my beloved region of Extremadura, although you'll find it more in the south. I first encountered it when I was a chef, working in Cáceres. I made it for my family once, and now we have it regularly – it goes really well with my honey ice cream (page 199).

CRUST

190 g (6½ oz/1½ cups) plain (all-purpose) flour, plus extra for dusting
pinch of fine sea salt
55 g (2 oz) unsalted butter, chilled
55 g (2 oz) good-quality lard (shortening), chilled
45 g (1¾ oz) caster (superfine) sugar
55 ml (1¾ fl oz /3 tablespoons) cold water

FILLING

325 g (10¾ oz/1½ cups) caster (superfine) sugar
325 ml (11¼ fl oz/ 1⅓ cups) water
finely grated zest of 2 lemons
120 g (4 oz) unsalted butter, at room temperature
200 g (7 oz) ground almonds
8 free-range egg yolks
50 g (2 oz/scant ½ cup) plain (all-purpose) flour

To make the crust, mix together the flour and salt in a bowl. Add the butter and lard and rub them into the flour with your fingertips until the mixture resembles breadcrumbs. Stir in the sugar, then gradually add the cold water, mixing with a knife, until you can bring it together into a soft dough.

Turn out the dough on to a lightly floured work surface and knead briefly until it is smooth and soft. Gather the dough into a ball and flatten into a disc, then wrap in cling film (plastic wrap) and chill for a couple of hours.

On a lightly floured work surface, roll out the chilled dough to a thickness of 2–3 mm. Press the pastry into a 25 cm (10 in) loose-bottomed fluted tart tin (pan), then trim away the excess. Chill while you make the filling.

To make the filling, combine the sugar, water and lemon zest in a small, heavy saucepan over a low heat and stir to dissolve the sugar. Bring to the boil, then reduce the heat to low and simmer until you have a thick syrup. Remove from the heat and cool until just warm.

Preheat the oven to 180°C/160°C fan/350°F/gas 4, and place a baking sheet in the oven to heat up.

In a bowl, beat the butter with an electric whisk until soft, then beat in the ground almonds.

In a large bowl, whisk the egg yolks until they are creamy. Gradually pour in the sugar syrup, whisking constantly, then continue to whisk until the mixture has doubled. Add the almond mixture and flour and beat until smooth.

Scoop the filling into the prepared crust. Bake the tart on the hot baking sheet for 35–40 minutes until it is lightly golden and a skewer inserted into the centre comes out clean. Transfer to a wire rack and leave to cool in the tart tin.

Remove the tart tin sides and slide the cooled tart on to a serving plate. Serve at room temperature.

PERRUNILLAS

When I was a little boy – a cheeky little monkey – and we cooked perrunillas at home, I was never allowed to have one when they came out from the oven. I would always have to wait for them to cool down before I could taste them. But, as a naughty boy, I would wait to see my mum, Isabel, moving away from the kitchen, then sneak in to get hold of one or two. I feel a bit guilty now (just a bit), with memories my poor mum chasing me out of the house with her slipper in hand, but I did really enjoy it in that moment – and I think, secretly, she had fun too. Strangely enough, though, I never got ill from eating them hot like my mum said I would!

INGREDIENTS

150 g (5 oz) unsalted butter
50 g (2 oz) lard (shortening)
150 g (5 oz/generous ⅔ cup) caster (superfine) sugar, plus extra for sprinkling
finely grated zest of 1 lemon
3 free-range eggs
300 g (10½ oz/2½ cups) plain (all-purpose) flour
100 g (3½ oz/1 cup) ground almonds
1 teaspoon ground cinnamon
good pinch of fine sea salt
2 tablespoons brandy
20–22 whole almonds, toasted

Preheat the oven to 180°C/160°C fan/350°C/gas 4 and line a baking sheet with baking parchment.

In a mixing bowl, beat together the butter and lard with the sugar until really creamy, then beat in the lemon zest and 2 of the eggs. Fold in the flour, ground almonds, cinnamon, salt and brandy and mix to form a soft dough.

Take small amounts of the dough (about 40g/1½ oz) and roll each one into a ball. Place on the prepared baking sheet and flatten each one slightly. Once you have shaped them all, press an almond into the middle of each one.

In a small bowl, lightly beat the remaining egg, then brush the beaten egg over the *perrunillas*. Sprinkle over some sugar and bake for 12–15 minutes until light golden brown. Remove from the oven and cool on a wire rack. These are best eaten straight away, but will keep in an airtight container for a week.

THE SPANISH HOME KITCHEN

SANTIAGO CAKE WITH PX CREAM

My partner Peter loves to bake, but I rarely have the patience myself – I find it too precise and measured. I always enjoy the results of his efforts, though! *Tarta de Santiago* is a classic recipe from Galicia, and also happens to be gluten-free and lactose-free. I suppose everyone has their own version of the *tarta*. Peter says it's a bit like Welsh cakes. (His mum used to make the best Welsh cakes – 'It's the secret ingredients, Peter,' she'd say with a smile.) Peter experimented with different recipes to create the best *tarta de Santiago* he could, and this is the result: light, fluffy and moist (some versions can come out rather flat and biscuity). He served it at one of our lunches recently and it was a huge hit. The key is to use good-quality eggs, and to take extra care to fold rather than stir the ingredients. Peter serves the cake with a special PX whipped cream or ice cream – he sometimes even adds a dash of sherry vinegar. It's really easy to make, and I hope you enjoy it as much as we do!

INGREDIENTS

olive oil, for greasing
150 g (5 oz/generous ⅔ cup)
  caster (superfine) sugar
4 free-range eggs, separated
finely grated zest of 1 orange
finely grated zest of 1 lemon
few drops of natural almond
  extract
100 g (3½ oz/1 cup) ground
  almonds
icing (confectioners') sugar,
  to dust

PX CREAM

250 ml (8½ fl oz/1 cup) double
  (heavy) cream
1 tablespoon caster (superfine)
  sugar
2 tablespoons PX sherry

Preheat the oven to 170°C/150°C fan/340°F/gas 3½. Grease and line a 23 cm (9 in) springform or loose-bottomed tin.

In a bowl, beat the egg yolks with the sugar until light and fluffy. Beat in the zest and almond extract, then fold in the almonds.

In a clean bowl, whisk the egg whites until they hold their shape. Mix 1 dollop of the egg whites into the almond mixture to loosen, then carefully fold in the rest. Scoop the batter into the prepared tin and bake for 30 minutes until risen and lightly golden and a skewer inserted into the middle comes out clean. Cool in the tin for 10 minutes, then transfer to a wire rack to cool completely.

Make the PX cream when you are nearly ready to serve. In a bowl, beat together the cream and sugar until the mixture is just holding its shape, then beat in the sherry and spoon into a bowl.

Once the cake is cold, the traditional decoration is a St James cross. The best way is to find an image of the cross online and print it out, then cut it out and place it on the top of the cake. Dust all over with icing sugar, and when you remove the paper, the cross will remain.

Serve the cake with the PX cream.

ROSEMARY PEACHES WITH VANILLA AND ORANGE SHERBET

I think the first time I combined peaches with rosemary was at a friend's house in Provence. We were staying in a lovely cottage overlooking the Mediterranean Sea, where the rosemary was growing plentifully, and we'd found some of the juiciest peaches ever in the local farmers' market. Our dear friend was hosting a party, and I offered to do the cooking with our friend Mark Hix, who was staying there too. Mark created a lovely Moroccan-style dish, and, along with some other things, I conjured up a tasty summer salad that combined roast peaches, rosemary and fresh goat's cheese, garnished with lavender flowers and drizzled with good honey. This combination is a firm favourite now: it's like summer on a plate. Here, I've used the same flavours to create a fresh and flavourful dessert, pairing the rosemary and peaches with a creamy orange sherbet.

SHERBET

500 ml (17 fl oz/2 cups) fresh
  orange juice
200 g (7 oz/scant 1 cup) caster
  (superfine) sugar
300 ml (10 fl oz/1¼ cups)
  double (heavy) cream
1 teaspoon vanilla bean paste
150 ml (5 fl oz/scant 2/3
cup)
full-fat (whole) milk

PEACHES

25 g (1 oz) unsalted butter
2 tablespoons caster
  (superfine) sugar
2 tablespoons honey
3 rosemary sprigs, leaves picked
6 ripe peaches, stoned and
  sliced into wedges

Begin by making the sherbet. Mix the orange juice with 75 g (2½ oz) of the sugar and set aside.

Whip the cream with the vanilla bean paste and the rest of the sugar until it holds its shape. Stir the milk into the orange juice, then pour this mixture into the beaten cream and mix well until smooth.

Chill overnight, then churn in an ice-cream maker until set. Scoop into a tub and freeze.

To prepare the peaches, melt the butter in a saucepan over a low heat and add the sugar, honey and rosemary. Cook slowly until the sugar melts, then add the peaches. Increase the heat to medium-high and bubble until the peaches are golden and caramelised. If the syrup starts to crystallise, you can add a little more honey and a tiny splash of water.

Serve the caramelised peaches with the sherbet.

THE SPANISH HOME KITCHEN

BAKED ORANGE RICE PUDDING WITH STRAWBERRY COMPOTE

I know rice pudding is a traditional dessert in the UK, and is often popular after a Sunday roast. Peter's mum used to make a lovely one, to which she would add fresh nutmeg for a distinct flavour. But the Spanish love this dish as well. I often have rice pudding on my menus in the restaurant, and people love it. The way we always had rice pudding in my home was to infuse the milk with some spices and citrus, and then just slowly simmer the milk with the rice in it, so it was very simple. My recipe here may take a little more time, but really, it couldn't be easier. If you're looking for an easy dessert, this is it! I'm not sure if my mum would approve of this method, but I think it's scrumptious. There's nothing better than a dessert like this, with a slightly crunchy crust on top and that silky smooth, milky rice inside. *¡Aproveche!*

INGREDIENTS

unsalted butter, for greasing
100 g (3½ oz/½ cup) pudding
  rice
50 g (2 oz/scant ¼ cup)
  caster (superfine) sugar
700 ml (23 fl oz/2¾ cups)
  full-fat (whole) milk
350 ml (12 fl oz/scant 1½ cups)
  double (heavy) cream
finely grated zest of 3 oranges
1 vanilla pod (bean), seeds
  scraped

COMPOTE

300 g (10½ oz) strawberries,
  halved
juice of ½ an orange
150 g (5 oz/ generous ⅔ cup)
  caster (superfine) sugar

Preheat the oven to 150°C/130°C fan/300°F/gas 2 and grease a 1 litre (34 fl oz/4 cups) ovenproof dish with butter.

Mix all the rice pudding ingredients together in a large bowl, then pour into the prepared dish. Bake for 2–2½ hours until the rice is tender and there is a lovely crust on top, but it is still a bit creamy underneath.

Meanwhile, make the compote. Put the berries, orange juice and sugar in a saucepan over a low heat and cook very gently for 10–15 minutes until you have a rich, reduced compote, but the fruit is still holding some shape.

Serve the rice pudding with dollops of the luscious compote.

MENU 1

Hake croquetas 79

Patatera toasts with manchego and honey 132

Broad bean tortilla 32

Rice and clams 97

Natillas 190

SERVES 6

TWO DAYS BEFORE
1. Make and freeze the croquetas
2. Make the natilla biscuits and put into a sealed container

THE DAY BEFORE
3. Make the natillas and chill

ON THE DAY
4. Cook the tortilla
5. Assemble the patatera toasts
6. Fry the croquetas from frozen, allowing an extra 2 minutes cooking time
7. Cook the rice and clams

MENU 2

Pickled oysters 76

Bitter leaf salad and seared duck breast with an apple and bee pollen vinaigrette 142

Cherries in aguardiente syrup with pistachio ice cream 192

SERVES 4-6 AS A LUNCH

AT LEAST A MONTH BEFORE
1. Make the cherries in aguardiente

TWO DAYS BEFORE
2. Make the base for the pistachio ice cream

THE DAY BEFORE
3. Churn and freeze the ice cream
4. Pickle the oysters

ON THE DAY
5. Cook the duck breasts and assemble the salad

MENU 3

Creamy milk and roast garlic soup with green olive toasts 52

Shoulder of Ibérico pork with jewelled couscous 166

Tarta de manzana casera 204

SERVES 6

THE DAY BEFORE
1. Make the soup and chill
2. Cook the pork shoulder then chill overnight

ON THE DAY
3. Make the tarta de manzana
4. Heat through the Ibérico pork
5. Make the couscous
6. Make the green olive toasts and warm the soup

MENU 4

Cherry gazpacho 35

Cuchifrito with preserved
lemon salsa 134

Tomato, white bean and
pomegranate salad 58

Grilled rosemary peaches with
vanilla and orange sorbet 212

THE DAY BEFORE

1. Make the cherry gazpacho and chill
2. Prepare the toppings and chill under damp
   kitchen towel or in sealed conainers
3. Cook the pork for the cuchifrito in the
   oven then chill overnight
4. Make the salsa verde

ON THE DAY

5. Make the tomato, white bean and
   pomegranate salad
6. Fry the cuchifrito
7. Grill the peaches and make the cream

MENU 5

SERVES 6

Sauteed jerusalem artichokes
with Ibérico jamón and kale 60

Spiced braised goat with
aubergines 136

Santiago cake with
PX cream 211

THE DAY BEFORE

1. Braise the goat, cool and chill overnight
2. Make the santiago cake and store in
   a sealed container

ON THE DAY

3. Heat through the braised goat
4. Cook the artichokes with jamon and kale
5. Make the PX cream

INDEX

A

B

C

D

E

F

Originally from a beautiful village, Talaván in Cáceres, Extremadura, José has now lived in London for over 22 years, and is often described as the Godfather of Spanish cooking in the UK. He spent his early years training in the top restaurants in Spain, before becoming Head Chef at a Michelin Star restaurant called El meson de Doña Filo. After José landed on UK soil he spent his time working at some of London's most prestigious Spanish restaurants including Eyre Brothers, Brindisa and Gaudi. In 2011, José opened his first solo venture, José Tapas Bar on Bermondsey Street. José Tapas Bar is a small and cosy venue, inspired by the bustling tapas bars of Barcelona. The daily menu depends on what looks good at the market on the day and it also serves an array of delicious Spanish sherries to compliment the dishes.

Later that year, José launched Pizarro Restaurant also on Bermondsey Street. He named the restaurant after his grandfather, who had a bar called Pizarro in Talaván. The restaurant went on to earn numerous accolades including World Food Awards Restaurant of the Year, Best Mediterranean Establishment at The Food Awards London, The Rosette Awards for Culinary Excellence, Food and Travel Magazine's Best Newcomer of the Year and Best Restaurant of the Year. José went on to launch two further openings in the Capital: José Pizarro at Broadgate Circle and pop-up restaurant Little José in Canary Wharf. It's always been José's dream of owning a country pub where guests can while away the afternoons and evenings in good company next to a roaring fire. The Swan Inn brings José's family cooking values to Esher while maintaining a British Pub feel. José's most recent venture has been the opening in the Royal Academy of Arts in Central London. In early 2022, José launched an exclusive seaside property called Iris in Zahara de los Atunes, Andalusia, providing guests with the most remarkable and unique food-and-travel experiences in a stunning, luxurious setting.

José's five books all launched to great critical acclaim: Seasonal Spanish Food (Kyle Books, 2009), Spanish Flavours (Kyle Books, 2012), Basque (Hardie Grant, 2016), Catalonia (Hardie Grant, 2017) and Andalusia (Hardie Grant, 2019), and now this, his sixth, The Spanish Home Kitchen (2022).

José prides himself on taking traditional Spanish flavours and dishes and making them even better. This mantra of simplicity along with Jose's charm, enthusiasm and passion for Spanish food has led to José appearing on many of our favourite foodie TV programmes. A regular on BBC One's Saturday Kitchen, José has also appeared on Sunday Brunch, Weekend Kitchen with Waitrose, Rick Stein's Christmas, Food Network's The Big Eat and James Martin's Saturday Morning.

ACKNOWLEDGEMENTS

This book has been a real pleasure to produce and was made possible thanks to the marvellous people involved in creating it. Above all, it's a tribute to the people and memories I have mentioned within it.

To my mum – thank you for your love and extraordinary gift for cooking, for teaching me to bring out the best flavours, and helping me to appreciate where our produce comes from, and to remember that food and people create great memories.

This book could not have happened without the brilliant contribution of some first-rate and extremely talented people. Primarily, I would like to thank my partner Peter (also known as @peterpancontomate by many), for having been a continual support both in the kitchen and in the editing of this book. A combination of my Spanglish and my dyslexia makes my writing quite difficult to understand at times, but he knows me well and writes well too, so he was able to help me express what I wanted to say. Also, thanks to our lovely girls – Conchi and Pie, who, by harassing me take them out on walkies, helped me take time to remember many home recipes and all the experiences associated with them.

To my Family in Spain, always there for me. Love you all. Sorry that you couldn't make the shooting days Carmen – you were missed.

I have always believed that we are only as good as the people we have around us, and I am eternally grateful to be part of such a wonderful work family. Thank you to Zoraida for all the work you have done to make this book happen. I know it was not easy to get me to focus sometimes but you have done an excellent job. You've also handled the complex coordination of the project. Thank you also to Monty, my right-hand man, for keeping a cool head and running everything smoothly and brilliantly in our kitchens. To Valentina, thank you for your passion and commitment to quality, to experiences, and to the team. To Andy and Simon, thank you both for your high-level of competence and professionalism in your respective fields. To Carmen, thank you for your calming presence and rational thinking. You help me keep a clear head. To every single member of the big restaurant family across the different sites in the UK and in Spain, thank you. Sincerely, thank you!

For helping me articulate and structure the memories of food I wanted to include here, thank you Lizzie. For coming to Spain and cooking with me, thank you Hattie. It was a real pleasure developing things together with you both.

Emma, your phenomenal creativity, sensitivity and expertness in photography is astounding. Thank you sincerely for capturing the true essence of the most important memories I have of my family and friends, and the dishes we chose to include – you have captured them so perfectly. You are always such a pleasure to work with.

To Eve, Kajal, Emma and all the team at Hardie Grant as well my agent Borra, for giving me this opportunity and all the work you have done to make this book happen.

Finally, I'd like to thank my dear friend and true food hero, Claudia Roden, for your kindness and your amazing, heartfelt quote – it is humbling and extremely touching.

This book is primarily a recipe book but is also a book about memories. I would need a whole other book to acknowledge everyone that has been part of my life, so if you have been, thank you!

Published in 2022 by Hardie Grant Books,
an imprint of Hardie Grant Publishing

Hardie Grant Books (London)
5th & 6th Floors
52–54 Southwark Street
London SE1 1UN

Hardie Grant Books (Melbourne)
Building 1, 658 Church Street
Richmond, Victoria 3121

hardiegrantbooks.com

British Library Cataloguing-in-Publication Data. A catalogue record for this
book is available from the British Library.

The Spanish Home Kitchen
ISBN: 978-1-78488-447-5

10 9 8 7 6 5 4 3 2 1

Publishing Director: Kajal Mistry
Project Editor: Eve Marleau
Copy Editor: Tara O'Sullivan
Proofreader: Gillian Haslam
Design and illustration: Evi. O Studio | Evi O, Wilson Leung
Production Controller: Katie Jarvis and Lisa Fiske

Colour reproduction by p2d
Printed and bound in China by Leo Paper Products Ltd

FSC
www.fsc.org
MIX
Paper from
responsible sources
FSC™ C020056